… and I came upon the flames of doubt and fear for most of my life, but through faith, love, and a resolve I never knew I had, was able to extinguish what I later discovered was nothing more than an illusion …

—Michael K. Hirshorne

Taking a Chance on Life

BECAUSE A MIRACLE MAY BE JUST AROUND THE CORNER

MICHAEL K. HIRSHORNE

ISBN-13: 978-1-934198-05-6

Copyediting by Author One Stop, Inc. (www.AuthorOneStop.com)

Design and production by Joanne Shwed, Backspace Ink (www.backspaceink.com)

I would like to dedicate this book to my wife Jennifer (mainly for putting up with me while writing it these many months), my son Jason and daughter Brianna, sisters Lisa and Sarah, and my entire family of aunts, uncles (both living and deceased), and cousins. You are all master teachers, whether you are aware of this or not, and have been the inspiration for much of this material.

I would like to thank my parents Marc and Beverly (both of whom transcended this physical plane), without whom I obviously would not be around to write this book. I am forever grateful to you both, for you were also master teachers in your own way.

Thank you to Evan Pritchard, Joanne Shwed, Randy Peyser, Mare Cromwell, Gary Schwartz, Michael Lee, Daniel Gleason, Ann Albers, and too many others to count. You have all been instrumental in bringing this material to life. I am eternally grateful for your assistance in doing so.

Finally, I would like to acknowledge you (the reader). My hope is that, after reading this, you will be inspired to follow your dreams as I did, no matter where they may lead.

CONTENTS

Contents

GAMBLING ON GOD

A Bet That's in the Bag

From time to time, life awakens us with painful moments so that we remember to turn our circumstances over to a higher power. Some call it "God," the "Supreme Being," or simply an intelligent force in the universe. As busy and somewhat distracted humans, it is a power we seldom think about until our feet are in the fire, and we wonder how we are going to survive.

When the pain in our heart becomes great enough, we let go and let God take over the reins—usually because we have to. Once we do this, amazing things can happen to rejuvenate our souls and rekindle our faith. This book is about what happens when we take this leap of faith, ask for a miracle, and then get it—sometimes in unexpected ways. Ultimately, this rebirth of the heart leads us to take a closer look at ourselves to find out who we really are. We realize that we are much more than packages of protons, neutrons, and electrons that consume an array of toxic products. We are *cocreators* with God, helping to keep all of Creation going, with mighty and miraculous forces at our command.

Lisa, the younger of my two sisters, was just a child when she first encountered a pain that her heart could not bear. She was sitting in our living room, and our father Marc was upstairs watching television. Several agents hired by the State of New Jersey forced their way into our home with guns drawn.

"POLICE! Everybody down!"

As my sister stood there, staring at them with horror gripping her slender, little body, the armed men arrested our dad on racketeering charges and dragged him out the door in handcuffs. As the police car roared off into the night, Lisa stood there feeling very alone, knowing that it would be a long time before she would see our father again.

I had already "left the nest" at that point (being 13 years her elder) and was spared the nightmarish scene that my sister witnessed. She told me about it later, and I too felt a familiar pain in my heart. I had known about my father's compulsive gambling for most of my life, but it wasn't until I was about nine when I really began to understand what kind of an impact it was making on his life and on those around him. It started a few years after I was born and got progressively worse. I knew in my heart that the dam of secrecy, lies, and cover-ups would eventually break; it was just a question of when and where. I grew up feeling like I was living under an active volcano in the middle of a sleepy, little Jersey town three blocks from the ocean, surrounded by family and friends. That night, it finally blew sky high, and the damage was terrible, even though someone driving by our house would not see the spiritual devastation. Like so many great American disasters that happen in "Mayberry, RFD," it was invisible to the naked eye.

Lisa did not let that pain in her heart go unmended. Even as a young girl, she somehow quietly transformed herself into someone who could see the "spiritual side" in any situation, although most people who knew her would not find it obvious. Her waters ran deep, and she tended to keep a lot to herself. As I got older, I was informed by a psychic friend that Lisa was an old soul who had "taught" in a previous life (maybe a medicine woman of sorts). She still has many lessons to teach about love, compassion, and giving with every ounce of her heart. Lisa is a genuine inspiration to me considering all that she had to go through, all that she did, and all that she continues to do for others. When people say, "Give till it hurts," they think in terms of money. When I think of this expression, I think of Lisa. She gives of her whole Self and makes a difference when she does.

... "caution" is not the same as "fear." Caution will at least allow us to move forward whereas fear will keep us where we are, whether we wish to move forward or not.

My other sister Sarah, who is two years younger than myself, was also afflicted with the invisible scars of growing up in my father's shadow. Sarah tended to be the maverick of the family, and, if given the choice between the conservative route or the more risky, would opt for the more risky every time. Although there were few times where she tended to shy away from taking chances, Sarah could be affected by life's pitfalls just like the rest of us, which I agree can be kind of scary.

There were a number of times (as there are with all of us) where she didn't quite manifest what she originally had "intended." One night, while having a brother/sister heart to heart about a friend who let her down, I said, "Sarah, just know that if someone didn't come through for you, they were not the one who could have truly benefited you. Be thankful that you were 'blocked' from going further down that path. If you could have somehow convinced them to change their mind, you may have found yourself in an even bigger pickle down the road.

"This may have been a blessing in disguise. There are no coincidences. You simply need to say to yourself, 'God, please block my path from anyone who does not truly benefit me, and send me the person(s) who will help me fulfill my dreams.' Then you need to *literally* believe that this will come to pass. You may find that the person who can truly help you is right around the corner and might need to use some trial and error to get the hang of it, but it does work. You will always get what you *call forth* but not necessarily what you ask for."

Sarah got through it.

Living the spiritual life, we don't want to be afraid to roll the dice and get things moving. We want to take some *calculated* risks now and then, with the idea that "caution" is not the same as "fear." Caution will at least allow us to move forward whereas fear will keep us where we are, whether we wish to move forward or not. It is also a good idea to remember to ask God (whatever you conceive God to be) to show us the right way to go, the way that spirit wants us to go, rather than tell

God what our list of demands are or *the route that we expect will get us there*. We are wise when we ask God to show us the path. A bolder sage would ask God to block them from going down the wrong path, just in case they didn't get the message. That takes guts, and it's a risk worth taking, if you really want to be a winner in the highest sense.

If we are truly trying to work with spirit to manifest a better world, we must *believe* that God hears us. If we clearly and consciously ask for this "fail-safe" roadblock to appear, we'd better be prepared for the experience and be able to accept the consequences. It seems like a gamble when it happens, and when we agree not to fight it, but in fact you'd only be gambling on God—and that's a bet that's "in the bag." Guess what? These divine roadblocks happen anyway; with courage and insight, we can choose to see them as a blessing rather than a curse. This is an important key to positive thinking.

Meanwhile, as we are asking God to stop us from going down the wrong road and taking the wrong risks, we also need to ask for divine help to give us a "nudge" in the right direction, which usually turns out smoothly, or a "shove" if the nudge approach doesn't work. It takes courage to ask God to shove you in the right direction, but sometimes that is how we *find* the courage to take the bigger leaps of faith that life requires of us.

I had a strange dream in 2008, when so many of the old roadblocks were being removed or rapidly fading away in my life. I dreamed that I was skydiving (a great metaphor for my life). I had a rather tough instructor, who was barking orders at me just before we reached the jump point. I looked over the edge of the plane door to the earth far below but then hesitated. I froze with indecision. The instructor was just about to push me out the plane door when I woke up. The final decision as to what kind of chances to take—and truly what kind of person I was going to be—was not made in the dream. It was left for my waking mind to decide, so that I would never forget.

I decided that I was the kind of person who was going to "go for it."

Some would say, "That was just a dream!"

I decided that I was the kind of person who was going to "go for it." And, to quote Robert Frost, "... that has made all the difference."

"Sometimes," I said to Sarah, "when we are on the five-yard line and should be going in for the touchdown, we feel ready to give up, to 'settle.' We simply have no idea how close we are to the end zone! I'm proud of you for taking the risk of moving out west and starting over, even though it didn't turn out exactly the way you thought it would. Please know that I'd be proud of you no matter what."

We need to keep in mind what the late, great Dr. Wayne Dyer said: "When you change the way you look at things, the things you look at change." Live with intent. Ask to receive—not only for the Self alone but to empower others and make the world a better place to live.

"Sarah, nothing lasts forever," I continued, "including our present situations. If we were not so hardheaded and just let the universe handle our problems, it would not be half as challenging. I know with every fiber of my being that all of us will be just fine. We will one day look back and laugh at how much time we wasted worrying about all of this 'important stuff,' which will turn out not to be as important as we thought. It's just an illusion manifested by the E-G-O (Edging-God-Out). It doesn't want to let go because, if you *are* an Ego, letting go means self-destruction."

Every night when we go to bed and dream, we wake up fully aware that what we were experiencing was not *reality*. The ironic thing about this game called "life" is that we will one day *wake up* from our 70-, 80-, or 90-year-old dream and discover a different reality—one that transcends what we perceived as death. We "awaken" to this realization, so what does that say about the dreams we had while sleeping? (Can anyone say *Alice in Wonderland*? How about *The Matrix*?)

I'm still going through the process. My goal is not to be perfect but to be better than I was the day before. Each day can be a little bit better than the last, if that is what you expect. Ask yourself what you are so

> "Worry" is a reaction to something that hasn't taken place yet and may not *ever* take place. "Anger" is a reaction to what is presently taking place but is nevertheless still a choice. "Guilt" is a reaction to what has *already* taken place.

worried about, let go, get ready for some divine guidance, and expect the "un"-expected. It's never actually as bad as it seems and is really just a question of where we're placing our attention. To put it another way: "Worry" is a reaction to something that hasn't taken place yet and may not *ever* take place. "Anger" is a reaction to what is presently taking place but is nevertheless still a choice. "Guilt" is a reaction to what has *already* taken place. Your problems of the moment are just that: temporary. You will get through them. Besides, you can't change your past no matter how much you think about doing so. Make amends (if possible) for what you have done, and move on! Your future, on the other hand, is constantly changing based on your thoughts and your *beliefs* about it.

The only thing you have to work with is the eternal moment of now. *Right now.* It is your gift from God, and that's probably why we call it the "present." Your so-called problems are of this moment; they are temporary in nature, and you *will* get through them. Try not to fret about finding solutions to these monumental challenges we all go through; try instead to give them to "the manager" and see what happens. Do you think Moses and the 650,000 Israelites—when they had Pharaoh's army behind them and the sea in front of them—had it easier than you did? They somehow managed through absolute faith in the source that created them. Do you honestly think that this assistance is reserved for a select few?

My parents had separated but remained married. (Don't judge it; just go with it for a while.) Our dad Marc was falling apart health wise, and Jennifer and I were starting to run a bit low on cash. We were trying to help care for our mother Beverly at a time when Mom's medical expenses were far exceeding her coverage. Mom was in a downward spiral of pain and misery, feeling destined to live without hope of ever living "normally." Meanwhile, the doctors could find no major problems from her examinations. Mom was also at risk of losing her apartment. Jennifer wanted to ask for financial assistance on behalf of my mother.

I spoke to Dad, and he said that he would continue to send Mom whatever he could afford. (He still cared deeply for our mother.) What did that mean? He also said that he owed the Internal Revenue Service $600 and couldn't even afford to pay that. Our father referred to a nebulous insurance policy from one of his jobs, but his "companion" Joan was likely to get most of it.

"Try not to judge him, Jennifer. It is what it is! You can't change his situation, only the way you look at it. Just know that when the money is needed, it will be there!"

About that time my father called me, sounding more despondent than I had ever heard him, saying that he and everyone else would be better off if he left this world. He revealed that he and Joan were not getting along and asked if he could move in with me, my wife Jennifer, and my children. I had taken a night job at a Giant grocery store to help pay the bills and knew that this new predicament would put a further strain on my already difficult "situation" at home. My daughter Brianna came down with a virus, and my son Jason picked up an ear infection. What else could go wrong?

But there were bright moments all along the way. One evening, I came home still wearing my bright yellow Giant shirt and black apron.

Jason, who was just learning to talk, said, "Grocery man!" He looked happy. Taking care of food made more sense to him than accounting.

I smiled and said, "Yes, son. Daddy's a *grocery man!*"

Making a Difference

Solace is not something you find; it is something you choose. A gentleman I knew from my company had a son with doctor-induced cerebral palsy from birth. I had hired him to do some painting for me, and we eventually became friends. We confided with each other on a number of issues, and I decided that I would help him market a product he invented to help kids and adults affected by mental and physical handicaps. It gave me solace knowing that I could "make a small difference" and maybe even make a little money doing it.

Every day, I got up and acknowledged that I still had all my body parts, good health, and a nice home, and I didn't have to fish through garbage dumps to find my dinner. I found solace from that—or chose to find it. Most summer evenings, I got solace from watching a sunset in the park that was around the corner from our home. Whenever I spent two hours over a $3 breakfast sandwich with a lifetime friend and talked about life, I got solace.

Breakfast, anyone?

MY FATHER'S HEART

King of the Broken Hearts

My father's gambling problem came out of a pain in his heart, a wound he could not get at or wrap his mind around to heal. It just sat there, burning a hole in his heart until it killed him. That pain was the result of something very specific—an arrow of fate poisoned by guilt, which penetrated his very soul.

He never talked about it. Hardly anyone ever does. They just die slowly from the pain, hurting other people along the way, because they won't turn it over to spirit. Yes, my father hurt some people, but perhaps not as much as fate had hurt him—or at least he probably felt that way. He carried a hundred-ton, invisible elephant on his back. Rather than turn it completely over to God and let go of it, he carried it until it crushed him.

I wanted to know what had caused his destruction. The clues were abundant, scattered here and there, but it took years to figure it out. Slowly I managed to unwrap the brown-paper wrapper, like peeling off the layers of an onion, to get at the truth hiding in the center. What I learned will take some time to tell, but it will help you, the reader, see my father in a different light. It did for me.

My father was what you would call a "racketeer," but there was much more to the story. I have no reason to paint a rosy picture of him, even though he was my dad. When I was about 21 years old, he figured out how to open up many credit cards in my name, and then use the credit lines to finance the ever-growing expenses he incurred due to his under- and sometimes *un*employment periods. This situation left me

To be myself no matter what—that is *always* the ultimate gamble.

with a heavy mountain of debt—just as I was trying to figure out a way to pay back my student loans. I guess he figured that he would be able to make a few big "scores" and pay it back long before I knew about it. Unfortunately, that did not happen.

In order to "make things right" and repair my credit rating, he conceded some eight years later to let me sell a 3.5-carat, canary-colored diamond, which was given to my mother by my maternal grandfather Harry. I was told that it was collateral for an unpaid debt—a fact that now appears to be blatantly ironic. Be that as it may, I had to hire an attorney and go through months of phone calls and meetings with the lawyer before the "problem" was resolved. I guess you could say that (in a sense) my father had literally thrown me under that elephant. I was ruined by gambling before I would experience three decades of my life—and quite frankly long before that in a number of other ways.

This discovery was one of my first painful realizations, which in hindsight led me to a life dedicated to spirit and to the discovery of the true Self. It was a challenge that my soul chose to face in this life. In the late part of my 20s, I already knew that, to live the life that expressed who I really was, it would require taking a huge gamble. To be myself no matter what—that is *always* the ultimate gamble. To do this, I had to trust everything to God and not lose faith, all the while knowing that my name and identification were linked to tens of thousands of dollars in debt that my father "forgot" to tell me about.

I had to figure out how to live with a sense of freedom in my soul, even though I was literally born into slavery, like some middle-class, 20th-century Frederick Douglass. I also had to learn how to forgive, and that is a hard lesson to learn. Sometimes forgiveness comes all at once for no reason as "unconditional love." Most of the time, we have to carve it out by seeking a deeper understanding of the pain that lies inside the hearts of those who hurt *us*. Eventually, I had to try and understand my father in order to reach a level of forgiveness that really meant something.

20

Sarah, Lisa, and I struggled for years, trying to comprehend why in the world it had to be this way with our dad. Why did he steal my name—the name he had given me at birth? Why amass mountains of debt in that name with the credit cards he was able to get, gamble his life away (quite literally), and then, on top of all that, shack up with another woman while still being married to my mother?

At about the same time all of this was taking place, my paternal grandfather Saul was arrested for racketeering. Clue number one. He too had a hole in his heart the size of Giants Stadium, and nothing could fill it. He too felt that deep well of guilt and shame that was too painful to talk about. So he turned to gambling on numbers rather than taking the chance and gambling on God. I'm sure that he would have had better odds if he bet on the latter. Ironically, he just didn't have enough faith. I say "ironically" because Grandpa Saul was quite literally a religious man—an orthodox Jew whose efforts greatly helped in building the only synagogue in town.

My father managed to bail Grandpa Saul out of jail, but it was a protracted struggle. Grandpa Saul endured a lengthy trial, and it took its toll on a heart that was already in pain from a secret wound that was quietly destroying our family. A year later, he was lying in a hospital bed with serious heart issues. Grandpa Saul died there, with a smile on his face as he perished, thereby reuniting with his son—his *other* son Barry, my father's brother. Uncle Barry's life was snuffed out by a drunk driver at the tender age of 14, but that was just the tip of the iceberg. Like the mass of that iceberg, 90% of what was going on in my family as I grew up lay below the surface of the ocean, many fathoms deep.

Before Barry's death, we all had problems like everyone else in town, but we just coasted along, half asleep. That event was the catalyst that caused Grandpa Saul to change the way he thought about certain things, to look beyond the limits of this world for answers. It took the life blood out of my father, Grandpa Saul, and Grandma Bea; however, it did not dissuade Saul from talking to Barry's picture every day until the day he died.

Every day, Grandpa Saul would go into the living room and perform his daily ritual. My grandparents had a beautiful picture of Barry, which I remember from my childhood. The house was grandiose—a massive, old charmer in Belmar, New Jersey—and the memories are delightful.

For example, the week before Passover, Jews typically sell or dispose of all their chametz (leavened food or food mixed with leaven). Grandpa Saul would make an elaborate scavenger hunt with the "remaining pieces" of bread that he scattered the day before in various rooms of the house. He kept the house particularly dark, for effect, on the day of the bread hunt. I remember going around the house with a candle, scooping up the bread that Grandpa Saul had hidden. He would use a white-and-red checkered container and a feather (used as a scoop).

I would say, "Oh! There's a piece of bread. Scoop that bread!"

It is surprisingly one of the fondest memories I have of him.

After Passover, we'd go into the living room, which was like a museum. There was a baby grand piano, lots of crystal, figurines, and several portraits of rabbis and sages. The house had a wonderful musty yet pleasant smell to it.

At this particularly special time, Grandpa Saul would approach Barry's picture with a distinct and ever-so-serene reverence.

"Okay, Michael. We've finished collecting the bread, so let's talk to Uncle Barry and wish him a Happy Passover. Let's see how he's doing."

He would speak to the picture like I'm speaking to you, the reader, as if death could not stop the love from flowing. It couldn't, but his heart was broken nonetheless. After Barry's death, he couldn't live life—not the way that most people did. He couldn't cocreate a life with God that was anything like what it "used" to be. He barely survived.

Grandma Bea pushed back and became judgmental, which was her way of surviving. Yes, my grandfather got into a lot of "shady things," like my father after him. Although my grandmother loved my grand-

> **When you need guidance, don't be afraid to ask for it, but be ready to see the solution in places that may not be that obvious. Your job is to ask, not ask "how."**

father very much, she resented him and worried that her image as one of the town's most prestigious businesswomen (she owned a real-estate business) was in jeopardy of being tarnished. Grandma Bea judged my father in much the same way, as did so many others. Growing up in a small town, where everyone knew everyone else, it was difficult to see the whole family go through that rather than get help from people who knew how to pull them out of their tragic and self-perpetuating dramas.

In hindsight, each event can be viewed as leading to the next in one realm; yet, in a different realm, I see another piece of the reality *I was creating.* How do I respond to that? How do I react? I don't want to give power to such events, even though they may seem to create a chain of other events, but only to the extent that it leads to a point down the road where I can say, "Now I understand!"

I came to the realization that it's a divine dilemma/paradox where you let go and let God take over in order to finally "feel" in control. When you need guidance, don't be afraid to ask for it, but be ready to see the solution in places that may not be that obvious. Your job is to ask, not ask "how."

We don't know where these addictive compulsions came from. The propensity to gamble was in my dad for quite some time and in my grandfather as well, long before Uncle Barry died. In his younger days, my dad saw this behavior in his father and then imitated it. As life went on and events took place, such as Barry's death, such tragic occurrences could have made things worse. They certainly didn't help.

One of the ways my mother tried to pull my dad away from this gambling habit was to encourage him to work with me on my homework. I was struggling in school. I was dyslexic and couldn't read very well. I also had trouble with math and would write numbers and letters backwards.

My mother said, "Marc, you need to spend more time with your son. You rarely spend time with him anyway. Sit on the couch and do flash cards with him; the multiplication tables."

And, by God, that was all my mother had to say. Dad *did* do what he knew was the "right" thing to do when it came to his son or daughter. It wasn't just to appease my mom.

I don't remember a plethora of fond memories of my dad as a kid, but my father was certainly a tremendous family man.

"Family comes first," he would always say.

He didn't mind hugs and kisses for girls as well as for boys when he entered the room, but that was also part of the quasi-Mafioso lifestyle he tried to emulate. He would embrace the men as he entered the room, and it was fine. Family was family.

Grandpa Saul was "connected" to the Mafia, but very few people knew about it. He never wanted to make it a big deal for obvious reasons, being tied to a prominent businesswoman in town. There were times at his stationery store when he would call in a favor; he had some ties. My dad wasn't directly connected, and I'm not sure that he wanted to be, but he had that attitude. It was a little scary. My father was a rather large man (about 270 pounds) and not too tall (maybe 5'10") but very broad, so he had a tremendous presence.

One night, he was in bed, talking with my mother. I was playing with Sarah near the steps, and she accidentally slipped and fell down the steps. We fought a lot, but I hadn't pushed her, certainly not that time; she just fell. My father heard her fall, and suddenly this huge man got out of bed and started barreling down the hallway. At 270 pounds, he sounded like a charging rhino. I was scared for my life, but my mother knew what had happened. Maybe she had been near the top of the steps and saw, but she grabbed my father as he barreled past her.

"No, Marc! Michael didn't push her!"

I thought, "That's it. My life is over!"

Mom saved me from *certain* transformation to the ... uh ... "nonphysical."

The Law of Attraction is immutable and just as powerful (if not more so) when invoked using the subconscious mind.

Looking back, I wonder if my dad really did have some connection to the crime world because I heard that he had a gun pointed to his head at one point. That's how close he was. He owed somebody money, and it got messy. In fact, he lent money to a lot of people; if they didn't pay him back, he threatened to shake them up. This doesn't mean there was a direct link. He had several different job locations: Two Guys, a small retail outlet; antique stores; other retail stores on and off; and a drug store with his boss—a small operation, with "shady stuff" going on that brought in a lot of money.

Dad tried to look like a high roller, even when the dice weren't going his way. He had whitewall tires on his Pontiac, which had a big point on the front. The car would be simonized almost weekly, but it was a façade. Dad enjoyed his life, but it was a tough struggle for him. He appeared to have all this money, but he was constantly behind the eight ball, running after it. The money seemed to leave as soon as it would come in. It was a never-ending cycle of chase, lose, and chase some more. The Law of Attraction is immutable and just as powerful (if not more so) when invoked using the subconscious mind.

He wasn't trying to make people think he was connected to the Mafia; he just wanted to show that he was the kind of guy who could make things happen. Pop was enthralled with movies like *The Godfather.* He bragged about how his dad could have "pulled in a favor" if he wanted to but never really did anything too "Hollywood" or over the top. My father, on the other hand, could make things happen in a mellow or nonchalant sort of way, like a dapper character in a crime movie. Grandpa Saul, however, never had the pizzazz of a Mafia type; he didn't want to be "the Don." (More than likely, though, he *knew* the Don!) When my dad had money, he would buy nice things; when he was behind, he would come home talking about "doing the deal" and getting it back.

Much of the time, my father was not in a good "space." He'd been that way most of his life, but that didn't mean we had to judge him for it as a family. He beat himself up so much that happiness was nothing more than a concept to him—one to be experienced by others but never himself. We didn't have to accept what he did, but we also needed to let go of the anger, bitterness, and judgment. What must it feel like to be ostracized by your whole family? Add to that the one-two punch of poverty and depression, and you have a miserable soul with nothing to feel good about.

Dad did this to himself, and that is a truth I can't change. I could have, however, changed the way I looked at the situation and thanked God that this was not me! I was able to give him a wee bit of happiness and call now and again, even for a few minutes, knowing that I would hear the same things over and over again. I learned to accept it, happy to know that I could continue with my life, grateful for the relatively good one that I had, and grateful that he and my mother gave life to me and my siblings in the first place.

Sarah told me that I was on a "forgiving path" and was proud of me for following it, challenging as it was for her to do the same. Sarah was not looking back. She was looking forward to creating a life full of abundance, a dream life we all so much deserved.

Sarah said, "It's our turn to prosper and share our wealth of knowledge with those around us."

I agreed wholeheartedly and challenge you, the reader, to be open to these concepts:

- Worry less, and enjoy the moment more.
- React less, and allow more.
- Do less, and be more.
- Whatever needs to get done will get done, if that is your will.
- It does not have to be a struggle.
- Think about what you are grateful for, and it will expand.
- Think about what you are lacking, and *that* will expand.
- You are loved more than you know.
- You are blessed more than you can presently perceive.

In August 2007, I got a phone call from my father. He said that his car had broken down and the cost of repair would run at least $700. I swore to myself that I would never let him borrow another dime. The memory of the day—when I had to hock my mother's diamond heirloom to pay for the massive amount of credit card debt that my father had acquired by stealing my name—came flooding through.

I slowly and hesitantly responded, "I can't give you much because my car is about to go, and I'm still trying to pay down those credit cards. How about $200?"

"Whatever you can do, son. I sure would appreciate it. I love you!"

"I'll overnight it and have it to you by Monday." I just couldn't conjure up the words, "I l-o-v-e you." I hung up the telephone and left my office to buy some bottled water. I thought, "Oh, boy. If Jennifer ever finds out, I'm a dead man!"

Just before getting into my car, I looked up at the sky and asked God, "How am I going to deal with this man? When will he ever learn?"

I sat behind the wheel and popped the audio version of Neale Donald Walsch's *Conversations with God, Book 3,* into the cassette player, and the answer to my question came right out! (I didn't realize that I had asked a specific question or was even having my own conversation with God. How silly of me!)

The message I got was, "Judge not the actions of others, for you have made the same mistakes, if not in this lifetime, then in some other one. Be not hard on yourself, for if you consider yourself to be beyond help, think again. God will wait for all Eternity for you to come back to him."

I guess I had my answer. It seemed miraculous, but why was I surprised? I should have been used to it by now. I quickly reminded myself that I was gaining a broader perspective on how such things worked.

I changed my attitude, and spun the wheel of life again with new hope, willing to take a chance on this old world because. . . . you never know.

I made it to the grocery store, got out of the car, and looked down. Next to the car, still in one piece, I saw a lottery ticket with the words "Mega Millions ... let yourself play." Me, take a chance on life? Just for fun, I played the numbers on the ticket. As it turned out, I did not hit the jackpot or even a few numbers. The point is that I changed my attitude, and spun the wheel of life again with new hope, willing to take a chance on this old world because ... you never know.

I couldn't change my dad, but I could change myself. I couldn't change the situation, but I could change how I reacted to the situation. If I acted with resentment, I would fuel the fire, which in turn would breed more resentment. I decided that, instead of "wishing" things were better and constantly brooding on that feeling, that emotion, and that passive wishfulness, I would envision things as *getting* better—a totally different thing.

Another quote from *Conversations with God* flashed across my mind: "The universe will never give you what you *want*, but will always give you what you call forth." [Emphasis added.] I decided that I would put faith in this principle of visualizing and allow myself to *feel thankful* that things were already starting to improve. I began to actually feel that they were changing for the better and in fact could see that transformation in my mind's eye, which is where the future takes shape.

I decided to know with every fiber of my being that I could create an environment of cooperation, helpfulness, and abundance. When I did this, change would have to occur, because I called it forth. Instead of just asking God, "How am I going to deal with this man?" I could have also asked for the abundance to help him. We always have a *choice*. If you don't like your choices, create new ones.

Spirituality and entrepreneurship are not necessarily mutually exclusive. When God is your business partner, things flow with divine grace. Isn't it better to think "outside the box" and forge your own path by ponying up with the One who gave Moses all his best ideas at that summit conference on Mount Sinai? With spirit moving us, we *can* move forward and manifest abundance 10 times faster. Money does not have to be a "dirty looker," "the root of all evil," or something that does nothing but "burn a hole in one's pocket."

Instead of saying to yourself, "I want to be filthy rich," rephrase that into a spiritual affirmation such as, "I choose to be blessedly rich!" This kind of richness helps you stand in your truth, and truth is a possession that no one can take away from you!

Money can be used as a tool, just like an axe. You can chop wood with it, so that the wood can be used to heat your home, or use it to murder someone. The axe doesn't care how you use it because it is neutral. It's happy to oblige you either way. What outcomes do you want to see and live with the rest of your life? The karma of a hero, or a villain to be reviled and feared by everyone you meet? The axe may not care, but *you* definitely should.

Money can take you either way. Don't worship it for its own sake; that line of thinking will send you down a slippery slope, which might send you sliding the wrong way. Try to focus on what it is that you choose without attachment to it. Notice I said "choose" and not "want." "Wanting" sends a message to the universe that you do not have what you would like. The universe must oblige by sending back that same vibration (invoking once again the Law of Attraction). Combining spirituality with entrepreneurship is a newly emerging field that will eventually redefine the role of the American entrepreneur in society. Becoming successful in business will give you credibility when you espouse that you believe in the above premise. When you become more consciously aware, *you* decide how your life will unfold.

We often think of "sacrifice" as an unselfish thing, even painful, but the word means "to make sacred."

We often think of "sacrifice" as an unselfish thing, even painful, but the word means "to make sacred." There are many sacrifices made in the *Torah* (the Old Testament), but they usually turn out well. Seen correctly, it is just an exchange, a trade, a down payment on a miracle. They don't always happen in a ritual. They happen whenever we let go of the past and embrace the next step.

I'll never forget the day that I had to give up my old Volvo station wagon. I felt sad, yet there was another part of me that was delighted and liberated because someone less fortunate was about to get a little surprise. It corresponded with a change of work and, as the tow truck came to take away the Volvo, I started thinking about the 20 years I put in with that company. It looked like the person who had been so averse to change was about to change everything in his life at once, and I had a feeling it would be soon. It also felt liberating to be free of the old limitations that had built up over time. Like an old man preparing to die and enter Heaven, I was about to get a new set of wings. I just didn't know what color. The thought of leaving my job was scary and exciting. I had the same job for so long that I had started to identify myself as "that work I did for a living" rather than who I was.

When I made small talk with people, the topic would nearly always revert back to the question, "So, what do you *do*?"

This would trigger a regression into the box of explaining myself in relationship to money: "I'm an accountant for a telecommunications company."

Each time I said that, I felt myself contract on a gut level and my spirit recoil within me. The contradiction between what my mouth was uttering and what my essence was feeling would become painfully obvious.

I wanted to scream, "I'm *not* an accountant! I'm a multifaceted human being who has much more to offer than my ability to reconcile cash reports and general ledger accounts!"

30

My *Ego*, however, said that I needed to continue playing the role that society expected me to play if I was to survive.

I was done living the lie. I knew in my heart of hearts that I would need to change my mindset if I were to get out of my comfort zone and create like I'd never created before. I was determined not to live another 20 years of quiet desperation and was about to place the ultimate bet of taking a chance on life. It was time to take a leap of faith and gamble it all on God.

I was "all in."

Faced with the possibility of living out my fantasies (even if it meant doing so with every spare minute of time that I had), and do what I was placed on this earth to do, I would fulfill my soul's highest purpose. I would climb up the mountain of life until I reached the summit, and proclaim to the world that "I am!" My intention was clear: Continue what I was doing while asking for guidance as to what my next "steps" in this emerging field of spiritual entrepreneurship were to be. *Leverage the universe while allowing guidance to come through.*

We Are Not What We Do

We *all* create our realities, whether we know this or not. Some of us create with conscious intent; others do this at an unconscious level by default. The way we create our realities depends on "where we're at" along the path of consciousness. This is neither a bad nor a good thing; it just is.

After the average of 17 minutes of being introduced to someone, you may be asked, "What do you do?" Know that it does not have to mean, "Who do you want the world to *see you as*?" (unless you want it to be). On the other hand, when you live from the perspective of the soul's agenda (as opposed to the Ego's agenda), what you "do" may be exactly the same as "who you are"; more often than not, it is. Therefore, relish the contrast that life seems to constantly throw at you. Don't admonish it! It will allow you to see with crystal clarity exactly what

> Life is a kind of trial and error. There is never an "end-all" or finish line but a never-ending series of creations. If you don't like what you have just created, no worries … create *again* and move on!

it is that you *want* and what you *don't want.* Do what you feel a passion for, even if that means doing it while you're doing what you *have to do* in order to get the bills paid. If 10 minutes a day is all the time you have, spend those 10 minutes with passion. It sure beats 25 years of ignoring your purpose on Earth!

At one point, I realized that I did not know myself outside of what I did for a living.

The words of poor Ivan Ilyich (a character in a book written by Leo Tolstoy), as he looked up at his wife from his deathbed, rang through my head with trepidation: "What if my whole life has been wrong?"

I have worked very hard to insure that this was not the case for me. In fact, it does not have to be the case for *any* of us if we follow our soul's agenda. This journey does not have to be at the expense of attending to our Egos; however, following the whispers of the soul could be just what the Ego wants. Do what *actually* "works"—not what you or someone else believes will work for you. Life is a kind of trial and error. There is never an "end-all" or finish line but a never-ending series of creations. If you don't like what you have just created, no worries … create *again* and move on!

I often thought of my father's debt as a burden that I was carrying around, like an iron tire around my neck. I suffered from it daily. One day, while walking from my car to the subway station, I noticed an ant on the sidewalk, carrying a rather large crumb. Normally, I would not have stopped and noticed such a small event, but for some reason, on that day, I did. I guess I needed to see it. I tried to think of why God made me observe this unusual sight.

It occurred to me that if the ant could carry several times his body mass and weight across that sidewalk, then we humans should be able to do infinitely more with what we were given. We should be able to move mountains!

I told the ant that I would make it my life's quest to help as many people as possible become aware of his feat of strength and of *their* own ability. It was a verbal contract. I didn't know how I was going to fulfill it, but, by God, I would find a way. We occasionally hear stories of mothers lifting cars to free their child trapped underneath, soldiers carrying their buddies off a battlefield on their shoulders, or rescue workers removing a collapsed house in record time after a tornado, to free a stranger whom they have never met. If those people can do these things, we can too. We are just lucky enough not to have the need!

Some may hear my story about how I grew up, about carrying my father's debt to the tune of tens of thousands of dollars, like the Greek god Atlas carried the whole world on his shoulders.

They would say to me, "I could *never* do that!"

Well, I hope you never have to, but the fact is that you *can* do things you never thought possible the minute you *have* to, as long as you have the faith of an ant. I'm writing this book because, in a funny sort of way, I am that ant—the ant who didn't say, "I can't!"

The Kabbalah, associated with Jewish mysticism, was first found in written form via a book called the *Zohar*—a bible of sorts, and the source of Kabbalistic teachings. The wisdom was passed orally from Moses to the generations that followed, until a man named Shimon Bar Yochai recorded it as the *Zohar*. It teaches that Satan (pronounced *sa-ton*) is ever present in our lives in one form or another. This "opponent" is not the same thing as that red demon with a pitchfork, horns, and a tail that we fabricated so long ago. It is simply an opponent who will challenge us to rise to the occasion when the going gets tough and not let our outer circumstances dictate the way we choose to feel about ourselves.

If you are waiting for people, places, and events to be "just so" before you can feel good about yourself or content/happy, you will be waiting a very long time! Feel grateful about what you have *now*, and you will attract more things to be happy about. There is *always* something to feel grateful about. Chaos, on the other hand, is invited into our lives in many different ways, creating an untold number of challenges, but the main route it takes into our lives is through fear. This fear leads us to react to life instead of being proactive, and then things become even more chaotic in a sometimes vicious cycle.

A little entity called "Ego" always seems to get in the way by causing us to take everything personally. At times, we are harder on ourselves than others would be on us. If presented with a situation that confronts our Egoic Self, we immediately feel the need to defend our position and offer excuses for whatever happened. The Ego wants to explain to the "other" Ego why we are right and they are wrong.

Listening to what the other person has to say, whether positive or negative, without allowing one's Ego to have sway can be liberating. When we refuse to take things personally—even things that may in fact boost our Ego—we don't get caught up in the "daily drama" and hence will not react to the everyday circumstances that present themselves throughout our lives. By being proactive, we reject chaos along with the repercussions of what reactivity will bring, namely more chaos.

My dad called me a few days after he had his gall bladder removed. I could tell he was distraught and angry before he even uttered a word, and I knew the conversation would not go well. He gave me the emotional experience we call "Jewish guilt" about not calling him to see how he was doing, even though I had called him on the day of his procedure and the day after the operation. The fact that he was sleeping from all the drugs they gave him at the time seemed irrelevant even though I tried.

34

> The drama in our lives can represent spiritual change and transformation, or it can be the result of our own desire for drama to bring attention to ourselves, like a young child who feels that their needs are not being met.

After being thoroughly berated and browbeaten, I finally reacted. I told him that he had a lot of nerve trying to throw that kind of guilt trip on me. I reminded him that I had invited him to my house on dozens of occasions, but every time he claimed to be too busy with work. I told him that I did not feel comfortable staying with him and his lady friend because he was still married to my mother at the time. Besides, I reminded him that, several months prior, we even discussed the idea of him visiting me after he recovered from surgery. The surgery got a bit complicated, which made him feel that his son should have been by his side, forgetting the fact that I lived several states away. I did what people do when they allow their Ego to talk for them: I reacted with anger and resentment.

Halfway through the conversation, I heard a click and then a dial tone. I felt angry and chagrined. I realized that I had hit him when he was down, and then let 20 minutes pass. After thinking about what we had both said, I decided to be the bigger person and call to make amends. I told my father that I was wrong for reacting the way I did and that I was sorry. In his own way, he accepted the apology. Carrying around guilt and resentment will shorten your life, and I knew that I had a lot of living to do.

The drama in our lives can represent spiritual change and transformation, or it can be the result of our own desire for drama to bring attention to ourselves, like a young child who feels that their needs are not being met. As my father lay in the hospital, Jennifer and I were undergoing major transformations in our jobs, and it was difficult to find time to spend with him.

At the same time, he and I were still acting out dramas from my childhood. I felt a hunger for attention, which was rooted in my earliest memories of him, for not spending enough time with me. This drama became palpable as I left him in that New Jersey hospital bed, heading

I pulled out my Zohar and prayed as I had never prayed before that the storm would stop and that I could return to my family in safety.

back to Maryland where I was living. The whole way back, I was praying that God would send me a sign that I was "on my way" to manifesting my dreams. I got as far as Exit 1 on the Jersey Turnpike, about a mile north of the Delaware Memorial Bridge, and the drama began to unravel.

Suddenly, a cloud formation appeared out of nowhere, seemingly in the shape of a hand, curling its fingers inward like some sort of a wave. Behind the hand were lightning bolts, and the sky appeared to have a greenish tint to it—a sign of a tornado on the way, some say. I later found out that the cloud formation was a supercell (a high-intensity, fast-forming storm). The cloud dissipated in a matter of seconds, and the sky let loose with the hardest rainstorm I've witnessed in my (then) 45 years on Earth. Hail the size of golf balls pounded my car, and a funnel cloud (that I could not see, as it was blocked by the bridge) started to form within a half mile or so away. I realized that this was not your ordinary spring shower. I pulled out my *Zohar* and prayed as I had never prayed before that the storm would stop and that I could return to my family in safety.

Fifteen or more minutes passed, but the storm raged on. I decided to cross the bridge in spite of the danger and slowly inched my way from the side of the road where I had been sitting to the far left lane. As I crossed the bridge, the rain started to let up. By the time I got to the other side of that long bridge, the rain had stopped. The sun came out, and the roadway was completely dry within two miles of that bridge.

I looked up and asked, "Okay. What was *that* all about?"

Just then, a rather large semitrailer going in the opposite direction passed by with a large sign that read, "You have just seen the future of your life." That certainly seemed like a dramatic way to end a conversation with God!

Although traffic was backed up for at least 10 miles on both sides of the bridge, I managed to make it back safe and sound. When I reached my home town, right at the traffic circle, I saw the most exquisite double rainbow I have ever seen. I took it as a sign that the stormy times my wife and I were going through would pass and that we would both not only survive but prosper beyond our wildest dreams.

Faith in What Works

I knew the end was near for my father but didn't know when. I didn't want him to die—that was up to God. If he had to die, at least I could perhaps find a way to help him go with peace in his heart.

Not long afterwards, my dad called me in tears, saying that his blood pressure was skyrocketing, and he was afraid that the doctor would not let him travel the next day to witness my daughter's bat mitzvah (a Jewish girl's coming of age) two states away in Maryland. I asked him to take a deep breath and have faith that it would turn out okay.

Immediately after I hung up the phone, I called a friend of mind and asked her to pray for my dad and do a healing for him. She had studied reiki, qigong, and a number of other metaphysical therapies and had been successful on many different occasions with healings from physical and nonphysical ailments and conditions. Unfortunately, she was booked until about 7:00 that night. I called my dad again at 4:45 and asked him to find a quiet place to lie back and concentrate on wellness and health—especially between 7 and 8 p.m., which was the time the healer would begin. He later told me that he was able to wrap a tallis (prayer shawl) around himself and start to pray at the exact time the healer began. I called Dad about 8:30 p.m. He sounded a little off—not excited but with a quiet confidence. He said he no longer cared what the doctor said and would come to Maryland, even if it meant he'd have to crawl on his hands and knees.

When I called the faith healer at 9 p.m., she was in tears. While she was sending the healing energy to my father, she experienced angels working on him through her, and that's when she started weeping. My

Make observations on what works and what doesn't work; from that data, make decisions as to what direction you want to go.

daughter Brianna's bat mitzvah was to be that Saturday—the first time in 50 years that a woman would be admitted in our synagogue to the bimah (podium) to read from the *Torah*. Prior to this date, it had been reserved for men only.

Dad made it to the ceremony, and he seemed exceedingly proud of himself and his granddaughter. It was a very positive, faith-affirming moment for him and for my daughter, who subsequently developed a devoutly Jewish perspective on things and maintains that perspective to this day. Although I do not share Brianna's perspective, I admire her tenacity, passion for learning, and burning desire to do good in the world. My daughter has a smile that could light up any room, no matter how dark, and my wife and I are extremely proud of her.

In the days following the bat mitzvah, my dad continued to struggle with faith and trust. Most of what I said about having faith in the process did not inspire him.

"Just because you don't understand the way something works does not mean you can discount it, Dad. You may not understand the way a cell phone, computer, or microwave works, but you use them daily and believe in their technology."

I tried to explain that spiritually we should try to do the same thing: Make observations on what works and what doesn't work; from that data, make decisions as to what direction you want to go. I have discovered that, by opening my mind to new experiences, by studying certain philosophies, and by knowing with certainty that I can be the cause of my experiences instead of being a victim of them, I can move through life with more grace. I can then have the energy to do what I *choose* to do, react less and "proact" more, have more abundance, and feel great about myself. If you can say the same, you should continue what you're doing. If not, you might want to try *what works* rather than restrict yourself (by habit or custom), or do what others say might work based on marketing, religion, etc.

A few weeks later, while at work, I got a call from Joan.

"Your dad just had a heart attack. He's still alive, but you better come quick."

I hung up the phone and quickly walked into my boss's office. He could tell by the look on my face that something was wrong. Before I could get the words out of my mouth, he was ushering me out of his office and telling me to just *go*. I don't remember packing as the next few hours seemed surreal.

On the way back to Jersey, I got a call on my cell phone from my dad. I was within 30 minutes of the hospital where my father was having his operation.

"Hi, son. I just wanted to let you know that I am about to go into surgery."

I hesitated and said, "You have to *want* this, Pop."

The response came slowly and, after a protracted sigh, he said, "I'm really tired, Mike. I have to go into surgery now. I love you."

"Dad, I'm only 30 minutes away. *Do you want this?*"

"I have to go, Mike. The doctor is wheeling me in."

After what seemed like an eternity in surgery—but only about four hours—the surgeon emerged from the operating room. He was supposedly one of the best cardiac surgeons in the state, but he spoke sadly, in a downcast manner.

"I tried everything I knew to save your dad, but the tissue surrounding his heart was as thin as tissue paper. I had nothing to work with. I'm very sorry."

Joan let out a wail and started sobbing uncontrollably. It would be a long day.

We had a wonderful memorial service, and I was asked to write a eulogy that expressed what his life was about—an impossible task. It occurred to me that, for all his faults, he tried to do good things in his life. In fact, not only good things, but great, over-the-top, *fantastic* things.

He loved the game of baseball, so much so that I think it might have even been his first word! Dad would beam with pride when he would recount the day he tried out for the (then Brooklyn) Dodgers at Ebbets Field. He would tell that story over and over again, but we loved hearing it. Because he was always struggling financially, he often said that all he had to do was "hit a home run," and we'd all be set for life. In fact, he was always trying to hit that grand slam, even with no one on base. We all loved him for that; he was such a kid at heart. He never hit that home run financially, but in his last days I tried to convince him that he had hit many home runs as a family man and as my father.

Here is the eulogy I finally read, after much soul searching:

The Home Run

A man lives out the scope of his days in bright sunshine but often in haze. We struggle, we anguish, we persevere, and sometimes a glorious rainbow appears. Then again, sometimes it doesn't.

When you attempt to hit a baseball and, instead of hitting a home run you barely produce foul tips, you haven't failed. You simply produced a result. My dad never gave up on hitting that ball. He saw it in his mind's eye as careening through the air after a powerful collision with the bat and landing somewhere at the 450 marker, way up in the top rows of the stand. A grand slam!

He would often say, "If I only hit the lottery, you kids would all be taken care of for the rest of your lives." Well, if anyone was wondering, that jackpot always eluded him. With the countless attempts at hitting that pesky little ball, he never connected with it in such a way as to produce his treasured home run. I do, however, give Pop credit for even attempting to hit the ball in the first place, and even more for attempting to hit it until the last breath left his body.

Dad, you didn't do things the way other people "thought" you should do them, but you did your best. You didn't have all the answers, but you gave it what you had to give. In the face of calamity, heartache, and pain that would have sent most of us running for cover, you showed me (believe it or not) how to stand up to it and face it head on. In spite of the constant struggles and the never-ending turmoil, you faced the music with dignity and grace.

You also never turned your back on people, even though some may have turned their back on you. You always taught me that, no matter what happens, FAMILY COMES FIRST. When you had a little "something" to give, you gave it without hesitation to just about anyone who needed it. You even did that (like Grandpa Saul) when you didn't have it to give.

Dad, you left this physical plane thinking that you never hit that grand-slam homer, which you so desperately wanted to hit. I beg to differ. I see a man who created a beautiful family, which extends to seven grandchildren and one day to great-grandchildren. This family, along with the extended family you shared with Joan, loved you very much, and all the jackpots in the world cannot replace that love. You did hit that home run, which always seemed to elude you, and now you know that.

Rest in peace, now that you finally can.
We love you.

Taken around a week after Dad passed.
Ball of light not visible in lens.

THE WOUNDS WE DON'T SEE

Behind the Scenes

October 18th had long been the date of Grandpa Harry's wedding anniversary. It had been a happy marriage. The one glaringly obvious challenge, however, that both Grandpa Harry and Grandma Shirley had to overcome was my grandfather's blindness by the time he reached 40.

After working as a professional musician and then a butcher for many years, Grandpa Harry had to find a new career. He learned how to become a masseur and eventually built up a fairly large clientele for a number of wealthy clients. In those days, it was not only acceptable but even expected for masseurs to work on clients at their private residences.

On October 18, 1962, my mother, after only one year of marriage, presented her mother—Grandma Shirley—with an unusual anniversary present: me. Shirley got her first look at me in the maternity ward of the hospital. While I was still in the hospital, news hit the airwaves about something called the "Cuban Missile Crisis," but our optimism in America's future and our own was hardly wrinkled. The "stare down" between Fidel Castro and John Kennedy ended with the withdrawal of nuclear weapons from Cuba.

The first months of my new adventure were rather typical for a child born into a conventional New Jersey resort town. Then, at four months, lightning struck. We encountered our own "Cuban Missile Crisis," and it struck hard and deep, causing some to turn to the guiding light of God's mercy and some to turn to the darkness within.

Dotty's life, along with the lives of my entire family, were turned upside down within four minutes on that horrific day in April 1963.

As with many couples, my mother's relationship with her mother-in-law—Grandma Bea—was a bit strained at times. For the first few months at least, my mother managed to make it work for all concerned. For some reason, she decided to trust Grandma Bea to babysit me while she went out to dinner with my dad for a much-needed break. There was no one else available; it would only be for a few hours. *What could happen?*

I was a bit colicky that day, much to Grandma Bea's dismay. About two hours in, I started to get pretty restless. She got nervous and decided to call her younger son Barry to come over and console me. Uncle Barry had a certain way with me and was usually able to settle me down. He had been "hanging out" (this was the '60s, as you recall) with his friend Kevin. Barry came as fast as he could on his bike. Not to leave a friend out of the picture, he took Kevin with him, a last-minute decision that seemed like a "yes" at the time but which probably should have been a "no." They rode doubles together, with Kevin riding on the handlebars, facing Barry. It was certainly risky behavior, but life in suburbia was boring enough. They headed for my house, where Grandma Bea was anxiously awaiting them.

A block before they reached my house, a drunk driver barreled down the street at a high rate of speed just as Uncle Barry and Kevin were entering traffic from a side street. Uncle Barry could not see or steer as well as he would have if he were alone. He saw the car and pushed Kevin off the handlebars, but he could not manage to save himself. His body took the full impact of the speeding sedan and was dragged for an entire block before the inebriated driver finally stopped. At the beginning of the block, Kevin lay writhing from the pain of a broken arm; at the end of the block, Uncle Barry lay dying in the street. An ambulance came and brought his damaged body to the local hospital—the same one in which I had just been born some six months earlier.

As fate would have it, the nurse on duty was Barry's sister, my aunt Delores, although everyone called her Dotty. She and the whole team of medical specialists scrambled hard to try to save Barry, but it was too late. His injuries were far too extensive for his body to sustain life, and he died shortly after Dotty had admitted him. At the moment of death, my aunt helped fill out the paperwork, and then declared that she was through with nursing. She quit that day and never went back.

Something deep inside her died along with her brother. That was the moment her heart was wounded beyond medical recovery. That pain was too much to bear alone. Dotty's life, along with the lives of my entire family, were turned upside down within four minutes on that horrific day in April 1963. From that point on, life would never be the same for any of us.

After Barry's funeral, Grandma Bea approached my mom and said, "If you hadn't asked me to babysit, my son would still be alive today!" My mother was *beyond* beside herself with guilt from that dark day in 1963 until the day she died, some 50 years later.

When Drama Does Damage

A s I look back on Uncle Barry's funeral, I think of how different my life—all of our lives—would have been if my mother had just found a way to resist being pulled into the drama of "who killed Barry?" Obviously, it served to heighten the drama of the moment to blame it on my mom, but it was a ludicrous accusation. Who among us could just laugh off something like that with a wave of our hand? Mom bit the toxic worm of shame—hook, line, and sinker—and went down like a small sailing craft with a large torpedo lodged in its hull. Her self-destruction was a movie we all could have done without, yet it was a lifelong learning experience. There's a reason for everything.

I thought I had resisted all of that. I did not feel that I had internalized my mother's pain and guilt over Barry's death and thought that I was the one who had gotten through it and toughed it out.

Spirit works in dramatic ways sometimes, and our lives should be the most amazing movie we ever watch.

In 2008, I started to experience what I felt was self-induced stress and anxiety at the workplace. I couldn't understand my emotional reaction to things that I used to take in stride, so I went to a counselor for a "checkup from the neck up." I was sitting in the chair, and she asked me if anything traumatic had ever happened to my folks as a child. I told her the whole story about Barry and Kevin and that I was that baby whose crying had triggered this incredibly horrible chain of events that continued for years.

While recounting this story, I suddenly felt Uncle Barry's presence. I began to sob so intensely that I couldn't even catch my breath. It was as if I had been blaming myself for his death for 45 years and never realized it. I did not hear him say this, but I felt his thoughts. He was trying to say that he was okay in the world he lived in now, and that it was not my fault. I felt so relieved when it was over that my symptoms lessened almost immediately. I had been looking for a guiding angel, and I found Barry. Perhaps there is another angel for me somewhere, waiting to guide me through life, but Barry has been on my radar ever since as a loving and wise presence, looking out for me.

Spirit works in dramatic ways sometimes, and our lives should be the most amazing movie we ever watch. I like my movie, and I often imagine it played out on the screen with the role of Michael Hirshorne being played by Tom Cruise, and a cast of Oscar-winning actors and actresses playing my family and friends, because life in the service of spirit is that "cool." But I never forget how damaging drama "queens" and "kings" can be, and how other people can ruin our lives by sucking us into their tragic "movie"—the one they keep watching over and over again out of habit.

My wife Jennifer became a senior manager of a company, which was a dramatic move for her at the time. What struck me as curious, but not surprising, was how hard it was for her to adjust to the heightened level of drama it brought into her life. Suddenly, all the movies of all the people she worked with became her movies as well and, for a short time, she found herself "playing into the drama."

"Honey," I said, "it's all just *draaaaaaaaaama*. It's not the event or situation but how you react to that situation. I'm sure you are doing the best you can. Don't try to please them all. It has never worked and never will work. You are the manager! Make managerial decisions, and let the cards fall where they may.

"I know you want to please everyone," I continued, "and try really hard to do that, but you can't. You're the boss, but try not to let your Ego get in the way. On the other hand, understand that your subordinates report to you, not the other way around. If you need to clear the air with a disgruntled 'senior employee' who's been there longer than you, then call her into your office and clear the air. If she doesn't want to 'do lunch,' then simply say, 'I need to talk with you for a minute. Let's meet in my office at 3 PM.' Period. You never have to let anything 'in' that you don't want to let in. Things will work out as you will them to."

Then I added, "You are an awesome mother, a competent employee, a loving and caring daughter and wife, a good friend, and a true soulmate to the one and only man in your life. You got lucky, but I got luckier. Move forward with the confidence that you can create your *own* reality, and make that reality anything you want it to be!

"I know things are tough, honey, but I am constantly looking for signs from the universe for ways to help improve our situation. I try not to buy into the fear and doubt that a lot of other people are playing into. I try to keep a good attitude about things, though the worst may go before me. What good would it do to think otherwise? Would it improve things one iota if I thought about them in a pessimistic way?

No! Things will turn out better than you can ever imagine. I am certain of this because I know that my thoughts can create my reality, and I am imagining us in a much better place. Know that *your* thoughts can create yours as well. Remember to choose gratefulness no matter what life throws at you. Think about Grandpa Cohen, a man whom you idolized. He lived in abject poverty but was the wealthiest man in the world as far as he was concerned. He was rich in spirit, and we can be that rich the moment we decide to claim that fortune!"

I turned to a favorite saying that just comes out of me sometimes:

We are taken care of.
We were taken care of.
We will be taken care of!

A Funny Thing about Money

As a kid, I was really mixed up on the subject of money. Everyone has a different take on what apparently is a subject that affects everyone on the planet, in some way, shape, or form. We had my dad, who was constantly chasing it, and working from job to job without health benefits. Our furniture was bedraggled, tattered, torn, and so in need of repair that I felt bad about bringing friends over. He was up; he was down. It seemed like there was no in between. On the other hand, I had Grandma Bea, his mother, who lived like a queen but didn't have a dime either until later in life.

Then I had my mother, who didn't talk about money.

Dad would be in bed with my mom, and I would hear him say, "You know, we have $50,000 in the bank, and I'll always take care of you …"

Mom would respond with, "You know I don't care about that, Marc. All I care about is our kids, and that they are healthy, and that everything is okay with us."

> You can do all kinds of things … but the only way you can change
> these memes … is to erase or record over the subconscious tape that
> plays in your head, telling you what to fear or feel ashamed of.

She had such a nonchalant attitude but couldn't really manage money or keep stewardship over it. She didn't want to. No matter how much she did or didn't have at any given point, it didn't faze her. Consequently, the money would come, but then find a way to just as easily … "go."

Then there was her mother, Grandma Shirley, who lived through the Great Depression. She had plenty but didn't have anything to show for it. Her house was falling apart, and she was dressed in rags much of the time. I remember little sayings she would share with me like, "Money burns a hole in your pocket. Money is the root of all evil." She had plenty but acted like she could care less. When she passed away, we found an envelope in an oven, which was stowed away in the attic. The envelope had the words *"For Harry and I to take a vacation."* It had $500 in it. Other nest eggs showed up everywhere—in Band-Aid boxes, behind drinking glasses, and even in a few books! How is a person supposed to have a good attitude on the subject of money when you are pulled in nine different directions at once as a child?

When I was old enough to realize what was going on with my father and money, I was determined to "make it." The words kind of rolled around in my head: "I don't want to just survive. I'd like to thrive!"

I thought, "I'm not going to let that happen to me! I'm going to move forward no matter what, and I am never going to have to worry about money or have the ups and downs that my parents had."

By the same token, a lot of these conflicting messages about money were downloaded into my subconscious, and they stayed there. You can do all kinds of things—workshops, therapy, affirmations, and so forth—but the only way you can change these memes (downloaded beliefs) is to erase or record over the subconscious tape that plays in

49

You create your reality through your thoughts about it; it's as simple and as complex as that.

your head, telling you what to fear or feel ashamed of. (Of course, now we can call it a "subconscious CD," but you get the point.)

Throughout my life, it seemed that the harder I worked, the more I got behind. When my son Jason was born with pulmonary atresia, I blew through a large pension in no time because my wife had stopped working. Not that I wouldn't do it again in a heartbeat, but it seemed as if life presented me with these ... uh ... "challenges" time and time again.

I imagined a little voice inside my head, whispering, "Okay, buddy. If you think that money is the root of all evil, and if you think that money just burns a hole in your pocket, I'm going to present you with life events that will reinforce that belief."

Your subconscious mind will see to it that you manifest events to reinforce your limiting belief system. From this premise, we can see how important it is to rewrite and rerecord these false notions we have about ourselves. We need to do this in order to change from what we believe is *inevitable* to what we choose is *possible*. From there, as we start to give more and more attention (and feeling) to these new thoughts, they become our reality. As Neville Goddard (see "Helpful Resources" on page 159) would say, we need to "assume the feeling of the wish already fulfilled."

Many of us say, "Woe is me. I'm going to be in this perpetual struggle, so I might as well accept it."

Baloney! You create your reality through your thoughts about it; it's as simple and as complex as that. It took me over 40 years to realize this, but I finally did.

With the medical and other expenses that followed the birth of Jason, I finally woke up and said, "Wait a minute. Maybe this is happening for a reason. Maybe I'm creating it unconsciously on some other level. I must want this challenge on some other level, to move beyond what I thought I couldn't move beyond before, and then move forward from there." This realization led me to write this book, to show people that it's *not* inevitable. It's not something you have to endure. You don't have to be a martyr; none of us do!

Many believe that they were born into these situations and say, "Oh, I was born into poverty. I was born into this, born into that …" And it's great to hear those inspirational stories about people who become millionaires after starting out so poor, but we reject these stories subconsciously and think, "It's just one in a million." We write it off almost immediately rather than take responsibility for our own financial reality.

I would say that I believe I have a great work ethic, and I didn't get it from my parents; I got it from other sources, which I had to find myself or which sought me out over time.

I was more or less raised by my grandmother, my aunt (my mother's sister), and my uncle. My mom would work on Saturdays and drop me off at my aunt's house; it was a close-knit family. My aunt and uncle lived on the opposite corner of the street, and Grandma Shirley lived next door. I would often go to my grandmother's house for dinner, and she could see that my mother was struggling but would never give her the opportunity to grow on her own.

"What are you eating for dinner?" Grandma Shirley would ask. "What about the day after that?"

It was as if my mother couldn't fend for herself. She was constantly being "smothered" by her mother. Grandma Shirley meant well but never gave my mom the opportunity to learn through experience. Consequently, my mother's relationship with her children later in life became an extremely codependent one.

From the soul level, we all realize what we are doing. We can either live from the soul's perspective or live from the Ego's. The perfect balance is probably not achievable; however, some balance can be achieved by consciously removing ourselves from that Ego perspective and allowing a higher power to drive for a while.

Lovable as he was, Grandpa Saul was involved in some kind of criminal activity; we're just not sure what. I am still trying to wrap my head around that fact. If I had the wisdom back then that I have today, I would think, "I'm not going to judge him for doing what he's doing." Maybe it was a lesson for *me* because my father didn't learn from it. Maybe the people in our life who cause us pain are the greatest master teachers we will ever find because they show us what *not* to do instead of what *to* do, and I did learn from that.

I chose to take the so-called "corporate route" instead of "let's do the deal, let's make the hustle." I'm not saying this is right for everyone, but at the time it promised the (false) security that I believed I was missing. We were such a dysfunctional family. Thank goodness Grandma Shirley was able to pull the reins in. She had some issues too, as we all do, but I did receive tremendous guidance from her in areas that my parents were simply incapable of giving me.

A grandson looks at the family elders and absorbs their ethics, so someone in my position had to decide if what those elders did was "right" or not. I eventually rejected much of what I saw.

Phillip, my scout master, took me under his wing. He saw that there were a lot of issues in my family, and he was one of my role models. My life was, and to some degree still is, all about extremes. Phillip had a touch of that himself.

He oftentimes would brag, "We're going to get the most Eagle Scouts in Monmouth County!"

**I judged my father for being a certain way, unaware (at the time)
that the judgment would come back to me at some point.**

Phil was a tough man—a former drill sergeant in the Marines—and
he kept that attitude. He once kicked a kid in the butt with his size 12s
for doing the wrong thing. (Back in the 1970s, you could still do that.)
I experienced this for a reason. I didn't know at the time why my life
had to be so abnormal. *Why me?* I was trying to be a good kid, get good
grades, and become an Eagle Scout. I suppose I did some things that I
shouldn't have done, but I went in the other direction. I saw what *could*
happen.

My father and grandfather never went to college, so I thought, "I'm
going to take the corporate route, so I won't have to owe people money
and wonder how I am going to pay the bills."

I wanted the steady income, the benefits, and the security that
always eluded us. I wanted to be the power guy. I judged my father for
being a certain way, unaware (at the time) that the judgment would
come back to me at some point. Most of us go through our entire lifetimes doing the same thing.

With all this confusion over the subject of money, it shouldn't be
surprising that it became a major issue for me as soon as I left home.

Jack Seeks His Fortune

In 1986, I moved to Maryland on a dare. I had graduated from the
University of Delaware in 1984 with a degree in psychology and was
having trouble finding gainful employment. I was still living with my
parents at the time. My cousin Cara was living in Virginia with her
husband Matt. Cara suggested that I get out of that sleepy little shore
town and live with her for a bit until I found steady work, which gave
me an idea. I started going through the phone book (believe it or not),
looking for companies that "sounded" corporate and had a benefits

53

package that gave me more than a discount on a pair of shoes. (Up until that time, I was an assistant manager at Kinney's shoes.)

I stumbled upon Wang Laboratories in Rockville, Maryland. After dialing the number, I reached the receptionist and said, "This is Mike Hirshorne. I need to speak with the personnel director about an important matter." They actually put me right through!

The personnel director asked how he could help, and I told him that I was looking for an entry-level position in the personnel department. After a bit of a song and dance about my experience and education level, the director mentioned that they were hiring order processors and invited me to send in my resume. Dr. An Wang had invented magnetic-core memory and sold the rights to IBM some years earlier. They were (at the time) the undisputed kings of word processing in the new world of personal computers. I thanked the director, hung up the phone, and felt my jaw just about hit the floor. I knew that I needed to put together a stellar resume and mail it (through actual snail mail) as soon as possible. *I didn't even know what order processors did*, but I had to take that chance and go for it. It beat selling shoes out of a mall!

After calling Cara and telling her the news, she immediately invited me to stay with her in Virginia while I went through the hiring process. A few weeks later, after completing the interview with Wang and several other companies in the Virginia area, I was offered the job as Wang's new (computer) order processor. I was beyond thrilled. The "chance I took" paid off, and I got ready to start a new life in Maryland!

After a few more weeks of living with Cara, I moved in with my aunt and uncle. I lived with these kind people until I met Jennifer—the girl of my dreams—some five years later and made her my bride.

My mom was tired of watching her friends move away and others get sick.

Gambling on Life

M y mom was tired of watching her friends move away and others get sick. Her entire family had either died at this point or moved away. Belmar was still her beloved beach town however, the town where she felt most at home, but it was lonely; besides that, she missed seeing her family. I extended the invitation to both of my parents to *move* out of their comfort zone, to where at least they could be with some of their family. While my mom was amenable, my dad would "have none of that shit." He was used to his job, his "ways," and his life as it was. Gambling on sports was one thing, but gambling on life? No way.

Dad decided that, if my mother was going to give him the option of coming to Maryland with her or staying in Jersey, he was going to stay put. He was so set in his ways that neither Heaven nor Hell could change his mind about how he was living his life. They still loved each other in a strange sort of way, but the trust that was once there no longer existed.

My mom figured that after a few days he would change his mind and move to Maryland. She knew him all too well. Those few days turned into a few weeks, then months, and then 18 years. My dad had long since shacked up with Joan by then. The affair was going on before my mother moved to Maryland, probably quite some time before, and we all knew it—even my mother! Mom turned a blind eye and ironically was happy that someone was taking care of her husband. God knows she was unable to at that point. The painkillers, sleeping aids, and numerous other drugs to control migraine headaches had taken their toll.

The triangular love connection, as dysfunctional as it appeared, seemed
to have a mysterious cohesiveness to it and went on for years.

A New Approach

Long after my parents had separated, and several years after I had
discovered spirituality and the intriguing world of metaphysics,
I called my dad and counseled him to some degree on how to get
on in life—even when the world had turned its back on him. I would
constantly throw out reading suggestions by authors such as the late
Wayne Dyer, Neale Donald Walsch, Deepak Chopra, and Eckhart Tolle.

I told my dad that I had forgiven him for what he did, and that it
was his life, not mine. I wanted him to know that I still loved him and
cared about him, but I could not bring myself to say the words. He
would often tell me how proud he was of me during those talks, but
I didn't know how to respond. I hated the fact that the world judged
my father as a black sheep and an outcast, and for a long time knew
that the world included me and my sisters in that judgment. My father
was disowned by the very family that he still loved and cared for but
who judged him until his dying day. His shame would ultimately run so
deep that it destroyed him.

Believe it or not, my parents remained married while my dad (with
my mom's knowledge) continued to live with another woman. It was
strange to the outside world, but it worked for them. Dad would even
send my mom money and little love notes with messages like, "Don't
tell Joan." Occasionally he would visit me in Maryland but in reality
would be "cheating" with my mother. If this wasn't so strange, it would
be laughable. The triangular love connection, as dysfunctional as it
appeared, seemed to have a mysterious cohesiveness to it and went on
for years.

My Amazing Mother

After all the hardships my mother lived through, and all the disillusionment, it became hard for her to believe in miracles, even though she witnessed them from time to time. I often felt moved by spirit to keep things positive around her. On more than one occasion, I felt as if spirit were reaching out to her through me. Sometimes I get this "plugged in" feeling where anything seems possible, and I just roll with it.

In 2010, I took my mother to the airport so she could visit my sisters Lisa and Sarah in Arizona for a couple of months. I knew that it would be a wonderful experience for her once she was out there, but the "obstacles" in getting her there were piling up, and we were running late. It usually took about 50 minutes to get to the airport; due to unusual traffic, this time it took two hours and 25 minutes. The plane was scheduled to leave at 6:30 p.m. My watch said 6:10, and we were still on the road. There was no backup flight if she missed that plane.

I got that "plugged in" feeling again and looked at my mother. "Do you believe in miracles?"

She looked at me blankly.

I continued. "You are going to make your 6:30 flight!"

Mom smiled, perhaps wondering about my mental state. We were able to get curbside check-in and a wheelchair, and then pass through security without missing a beat. She boarded the plane as the last passenger, with one seat left and one minute to spare. It was impossible, but it happened! She was happy to get to Arizona, and I was so inspired that it made me feel like telling the world about positive thinking and visualization—maybe even finish writing this book!

Conversation with God
via a License Plate

About that same time in 2010, I often listened to Deepak Chopra tapes and CDs, keeping my positive energy boosted, and for the first time heard Chopra's lecture on what he called "Brahman," which is akin to divine spirit or energy of the highest order. Just after listening to it, a car pulled in front of me with a license plate that read "BRAMAN." The spelling may have been slightly different, but the message was the same. We are always having a conversation with God; we just don't always get good reception. That's not God's fault, however; it's ours. When we choose to really listen, God will "speak," but it may not be in the way we expect.

Earlier that same day, I was listening to Neale Donald Walsch's audio book called *Conversations with God*, with Ed Asner playing the voice of God. Asner explained how God knew Godself conceptually before the Big Bang but wanted to *experience* this as the creator and the "created"; thus, God was able to experience the infinite aspects of the divine through the entire physical universe. He imbued us all with the same creative power—thus, the biblical reference, "made us in his image and likeness."

When I saw the license plate with the word "Brahman" (in fact, one of his 1,000 or so names), I took it as a reminder that each of us was made in his image and likeness as well. To me, the words "image" and "likeness" have been misconstrued throughout history. If the source of all cannot be divided, then it holds that its essence would be in everything we perceive in physicality. God's "image" then can only be defined through the perceiver. God's "likeness," on the other hand, means that we were created for the purpose of cocreating with the source of all Creation.

I was working on creating a life that would lead to the highest fulfillment of my soul while helping that soul to evolve. The decision not to follow in my father's footsteps, which had led him to a "House of

We believe that whatever we are thinking, others are probably thinking the same thing, and that this is just the way things "are."

the Rising Sun" kind of poverty and ruin, was a choice that was fairly easy to make. It was therefore interesting that I found myself "following" a vehicle that said "Brahman"—a variation on Brahma, a Sanskrit word for God (one aspect of the triune godhead), which means "vast." Brahman means "the impersonal ultimate principle" while Brahma Vihara means "a divine state of mind" in Buddhism. All of these words related to Brahman.

Baskets of Love

When visiting my mom, I was especially aware that I was no longer the helpless child I had been when my dad would come home broke and depressed. One of the things I would do to reinforce this unfearful, "healthy parent" side of myself was that, when I went to her apartment complex, I would bring baskets of food with me and deliver them to less fortunate people there.

It was amazing how grateful they were to see me! Whenever I took time from my day to prepare the gifts, those simple baskets brought out wide smiles and big hugs for me! It probably made me feel better than it made them feel, and I'm okay with that. It helped me forget my problems for a while and reminded me how good my life really was, that I could still offer a bit of food to someone else. It helped me "wake up" for a moment to a reality bigger than the one I was currently experiencing.

Most of us go through our lives "sleepwalking," without being consciously aware of what we are doing or why we are actually doing it, and my mother was no exception. Seeing me with the food baskets on those occasions may have alleviated her constant thoughts of defeat and depression. I didn't have to say much about those occasional times

We will then become more intimate with the illusion (from a different perspective), have fun with it, and play with it for a while—knowing that it *is still* only an illusion.

but would sometimes mention how nice it was to connect with her friends in the building.

We often take on the "collective consciousness." We believe that whatever we are thinking, others are probably thinking the same thing, and that this is just the way things "are." This way of thinking is a waste of time and offers little opportunity for learning or growth. Don't concern yourself with being the "maverick" if that little voice in your head keeps steering you away from what everyone else tends to be doing!

Other times, we walk around in a reactive, Egocentric state for most of our waking hours. The trick is to be as consciously present *in the now* as we can possibly be for the part of the day that we *are* consciously creating. Upon waking from our eight-hour reverie and seeing the sunrise, we realize that it was just a dream. To be attached to that dream is beyond absurd.

When we awaken from this 70-, 80-, 90-, or (dare I say) 100 plus-year dream, I think we will come to this same conclusion. I feel certain that my mother, now passed from this dimension to some other, is seeing things much more clearly—as if a light had been turned on in a dark room. Finally free of medications, pills, sorrow, and pain, she is probably looking back on her physical life and asking herself, "*What was I thinking?*"

Tools for Seeing

Soldiers use night-vision goggles to see through the darkness that blinds the rest of us. It is a tool that gives them the gift of sight. Some sages, spiritual teachers, and even "average, everyday people" have been blessed with tools of a very different nature—conceptual tools to help them see through the darkness that blinds everyone around them. These tools help us see through life's illusions, so that we can walk in wakefulness. In this state, we tend not to resist or cling to those illusions. On the flip side, *Conversations with God* points out that what we resist will persist, and what we look at (or rather see it for what it really is) will tend to disappear. We will then become more intimate with the illusion (from a different perspective), have fun with it, and play with it for a while—knowing that it *is still* only an illusion.

The book I mentioned earlier—the *Zohar*—preserves a piece of spiritual "technology" that goes back to Adam and Eve. Although associated with Jewish mysticism, there is nothing mystical about it when you discover its inner workings. It is a technology, plain and simple, and not necessarily Jewish. Jesus more than likely used the Kabbalah to perform his miracles, as did some gentiles after him, but so did a number of other "nonreligious" figures throughout history. Sir Isaac Newton, William Shakespeare, and Albert Einstein were apparently also familiar with the Kabbalah's teachings. Like the night goggles mentioned above, it is a tool that helps us see through the darkness.

I tried on a regular basis to mention the Kabbalah to my mother, just to place the word in conversation and bring the discussion into a broader perspective. I know she heard me and understood the general idea of what it was about, but something inside her was not ready to spread her wings and fly. She wanted to trust only in what she could see with her own eyes.

A great sage once said, "If you wish to *truly* see, you need to use more than just your eyes."

The Greatest Gift

One day when I was visiting with my mother, I decided to get real and get some things off my chest. When I thought of some of the things my father had put us through, I would break down in tears. I hugged my mother and told her that I loved her, that I would take care of her, and that I believed she got a raw deal. I felt that she did not deserve the life she was living—or should I say surviving?

"Mom, I am going to make sure that you finally start to live the life you were destined to have." It was obvious that I was emotionally distraught.

We hugged for a while, and then my mother calmly responded, "Stop crying, Michael. Your father gave me the greatest gift a human being could ever receive. It was a gift that no other person in the world could give me: you three kids. For that, I will always be grateful. For that, I will always be rich."

"I love you, Mom."

"I love you back, son."

At that moment, I realized that this sweet woman, with very little education, had more wisdom than any degree could confer. Those daggers of guilt, financial stress from the gambling, and anxiety aimed at her heart never killed her; they had made her stronger. She was very much aware of what really counted in this crazy world.

At some point in your life, there will be a moment where you just "get it." The question is, "Will it be in this lifetime?"

Mom had been hit by a car as a little girl and incurred kidney problems from the accident; at age 53 (around 1995), she received news from the doctor that she needed to have a kidney transplant or endure dialysis for the rest of her life.

We siblings talked about it, but Lisa—the youngest of the three—stepped forward without hesitation. She would have to go through tissue testing, which could be uncomfortable. Yes, it was a calculated risk, but certainly one worth taking if the blood typing matched up.

Lisa weighed the consequences and said, "Let's go for it!"

She gambled and won (for herself and her siblings) a few more years of having a living, loving mother and, thanks to Lisa's tremendous sacrifice, a relatively happy one. That was priceless to Lisa, and she

> **At that moment, I realized that this sweet woman, with very little education, had more wisdom than any degree could confer.**

never regretted the transaction or questioned the price of that gift. She took a chance on life, and it paid off.

My mother was in dire pain after having been diagnosed with sciatica and a herniated disc. The pain was so intense that she had to go to the emergency room. They prescribed oxycodone, which offered zero relief and a raft of troubles.

After she got home from the hospital, I started making lunchtime visits to her apartment, with words of encouragement and a few gifts of nonhospital food. I also brought her a *Zohar*; *The 72 Names of God*; Michael Berg's *Becoming Like God*; and, of course, the *Conversations with God* audio tapes. After a few days of scanning the *Zohar* and meditating on "Miracle Making" and "Healing," her pain went from 10 to about 4. She started sleeping better, waking up earlier, and organizing her apartment with some help. This was so unlike her, and it was marvelous to see.

After a period of time (regretfully), the pain started coming back. My mother tried to make an appointment for a cortisone shot only to be told that she could not meet with the doctor until October 14th.

"October 14th?" I asked. "Do you really want to wait three more weeks to get some relief?"

She shook her head and started crying. "Michael, what can I do? I've lived with one kind of pain or another my whole life. What choice do I have?"

"You *do* have a choice, Mom. You can decide that you no longer wish to be in this movie. Fire the director, fire the producer, and fire all the actors!"

I asked my mother if she knew how much she was loved. She didn't really answer but just smiled that quiet, humble way she always did.

I told her that October 14th was not an acceptable choice and to envision and expect getting an appointment tomorrow. We called the regional manager of the spine center and explained the situation. Two hours later, I received a call that there was a cancellation and that she would be able to have the procedure the next day. In other words, she became the cause instead of the effect.

I asked her to try acupuncture, but she continued to pop one pain pill after another like candy, and then sleep until five in the afternoon, relying on breakfast shakes throughout the day for nutrition. One thing, though: She cried out to me to try and finish this book before she went to see Dad in Heaven. I unfortunately was not able to do that. I hope she can read it from wherever she "is." I know that she probably won't need to read it; she'll just know it by heart.

In April 2015, Mom was in a hospice center (fairly close to my sisters) in Arizona, dying from Stage IV pancreatic cancer. She lived with a number of ailments in later life, including spinal stenosis, arthritis, and neuropathy. Just before I left to go back home to Maryland, I asked my mother if she knew how much she was loved. She didn't really answer but just smiled that quiet, humble way she always did.

She barely got out the words and, in an almost inaudible whisper, said, "The next time I see you, you'll be all grown up!"

"You really are something, Mom," I said as I pushed back my tears.

"Take care of yourself, Michael."

It was one of the moments with my mother that would stay firmly etched in my mind forever. I held her hand and kissed her gently on the cheek. Sarah mentioned that it was time to go, and I turned towards the door. We hugged each other as we walked to the car, tears flowing freely now.

Words didn't seem necessary, but I said, "She'll finally be out of pain and at peace!"

Sarah readily agreed.

After we got home we called Lisa, whose personal sacrifice had at least prolonged Mom's life a few extra years, and relayed what had happened. This apparent "loss" was a leap of faith that paid back in a trifecta of love, hope, and happiness.

After one more phone call to Mom, and after looking at a photo of her and her friend Marjory, I realized that this was the end of a chapter but not the story. Mom had some amazing friends—more like earth angels. We are all blessed more than we can imagine.

From the time my mother took her first sleeping pill (after Grandma Bea made her infamous comment about her son's death being my mom's fault) until the day she died, she carried a burden of guilt that would crush most human beings. From that point on, she became a shadow of her former self. She couldn't sleep that first night or for the days, months, and years that followed. Soon she was wolfing down sleeping pills and tranquilizers just to rest.

Of course, they gave diminishing returns year after year, and her sleeping pattern never recovered. She hardly slept at all. Mom would take a pill at 10 p.m. but wouldn't fall asleep until three in the morning. Then she'd sleep for an hour or two because she liked to watch TV *all the time*. It seemed that way because it was too painful for her to face the world, and suicide took the kind of courage that my mother just couldn't summon; she was trapped. What kind of life was that? Then she would sleep all day long, and then couldn't sleep the next night, which perpetuated the cycle. Mom, like most of us, was walking through life half asleep, pursuing darkness rather than light and choosing to live in a trance of self-induced numbness rather than awaken to the risky but promising gamble that is life.

She was in a dream that we *all* are in—*The Matrix*—and from which we will wake up one day, at the point of "death," when we transform from physical to nonphysical, as strange as that may sound. My mom actually "got" that she was in the illusion, in the "dream," and it

This endless cycle of suffering and numbing became a monkey on her back, which stayed with her for the rest of her life.

didn't matter to her. She stepped outside the box and transformed it in her own way.

I became highly judgmental of her at that time. "You're not eating right. You're not being productive. You're not keeping a regular job. You're driving us all crazy!"

But I know now that, if I had asked her, she may have said, "My life is meant to be this way. It's all for a purpose. I am teaching other people what not to do with their lives!"

I don't know if she was thinking that, or why these tragedies happen, but I do know that I learned from it. Who among us is really awake? I thought I was then, but I no longer assume that.

Mom expanded to other ailments. She developed migraine headaches, and the pain was so intense that she began using Fiorinal.

Her doctors said, "You can't keep taking Fiorinal or you'll blow out a kidney."

Well, the pain was bad enough (in my mother's opinion) to keep taking the pills every day, against her doctor's orders, and it wasn't long before she blew out that kidney. Along with this was a number of other maladies and conditions that gave her a reason to use prescription pain meds. After a time, this endless cycle of suffering and numbing became a monkey on her back, which stayed with her for the rest of her life.

When her time finally came, she said, "I'm getting tired." I was well aware she didn't mean that she felt like taking a nap.

My father said the exact same thing while I was en route to the hospital after his heart attack. An hour later, while on the operating table, he made the decision to transform his energy and be done with this earthly illusion of ours.

In the case of both parents, I believe they were saying this from a "soul perspective," and what appears to be blatantly obvious was that they had experienced "enough" of physicality. Their souls were unable to evolve any further in that incarnation, and it was time to transform.

In the case of my mother, it was actually a beautiful thing. I say that because the vast majority of us fight this process with everything we have. The Ego goes out kicking and screaming, but the higher Self is finally free of its prison.

Sarah was visiting Mom at the hospice center fairly early one morning, just 12 or so hours before Mom decided to leave this physical plane for bolder adventures. Cousin Cara was there visiting with Mom as well. After a few hours, Sarah mentioned that she wanted to "take a break."

"Let's go to yoga class," Sarah whispered to Cara in a hushed tone, so as not to disturb Mom.

Cara nodded approvingly, and they left while my mother was sleeping. At this point, the doses of Dilaudid were so high that Mom was in a perpetual stupor. The whispering gesture was more than likely not necessary.

After Sarah and Cara arrived at the yoga class, Sarah indicated that the instructor was not the one whom she usually had.

Cara was a bit perturbed. "I don't want a substitute. I want the 'real' one. Let's go another time."

Sarah paused for a moment and said, "Let's just do it. Maybe she'll have something to show us, and we'll remember to relax or something."

The yoga instructor started right away. "I want you to practice these breathing techniques. If you know anyone who has trouble breathing, I want you to show this to them and help them. Go through the breaths with them. Maybe there is someone you are thinking of right now who could use this information."

Cara just shrugged and said, "Whatever."

About four hours after that class, at 10 or maybe 11 p.m., Sarah got a call from the nurse on duty at the hospice center. "You'd better get over here. Your mother is having trouble breathing!"

My mother was (until her last breath) her typical, stubborn self and was waiting until Sarah got there.

Sarah knew that this was it. She drove to the hospice with Cara just in time, bent over, and cradled Mom in her arms. As my sister looked into our mother's eyes, time seemed to stand still; they both knew what was about to happen.

Sarah looked deeply into Mom's eyes and said, "Breathe with me, Mom. Breathe with me," continuing to cradle her.

My mother was (until her last breath) her typical, stubborn self and was waiting until Sarah got there. She *knew* she was being called home. We really don't know for *sure*, but does it matter?

As my sister cradled my mother and looked into her eyes, she said, "It's okay. You can let go now."

Mom had been struggling with rapid, shallow breaths. At that point, her body went limp, and off she went. It was one, big hug: the nurse, Cara, Sarah, and my mother.

When Lisa heard this story, she immediately responded with, "I heard Daddy's thick, Jersey accent in my head, saying, 'C'mon already, Bev. It's time to go.'"

That was an intense period; however, it was not as intense as what happened later. Mom was the first person to be cremated in our family. In Judaism, we don't normally cremate, but we didn't have much money, and the insurance money was not enough to cover the cost of a funeral. In any respect, Mom didn't want a funeral; she wanted to be buried next to my father in a cemetery that was already overcrowded, and there wasn't any room in my father's family plot. My father was in his plot, and his brother Barry was next to him. Behind them were my paternal grandparents Bea and Saul. There was no room for my mother; in fact, the cemetery was pretty much completely full.

Mom had said a few years earlier, "I don't care. I want to be buried next to Dad."

Sarah and I had said, "If she gets cremated, we'll take a little ash and sprinkle it over the plot."

My father's family plot

We cremated her, and my sisters and I came up with a brilliant plan of having a life ceremony. After my mother died, I arranged with the mayor of Belmar, New Jersey (where I grew up), to have this atypical "ceremony." Typically, it would cost $8 for a day pass until 5:00 p.m. I told the mayor that my grandfather and grandmother had businesses there, and all we wanted to do was have a life ceremony for my mother on the beach.

He seemed fine with that and said, "You can come at 4 p.m. and stay until 6 or 7 for free, if you'd like."

I felt like Moses, walking down the streets of Belmar with 45 people behind me in a big parade. We waved little flags so we could see each other (ironically in the same manner in which a funeral procession would keep its headlights on), and headed to the beach with my mother's ashes in a little bag enclosed in a box. It was a gorgeous, sunny day, with a slight ocean breeze, and we were surrounded by friends and family.

Walking to the ocean for Mom's life ceremony

The ceremony was powerful and moving. We didn't even think of it as a funeral; we were just celebrating the beautiful life of this woman. We had no idea that so many people would show up. They were her friends—from New York, New Jersey, Maryland, and other places. Friends from near and far all came to this ceremony. I had written a piece to read out loud about her life and how many people she had affected.

Afterwards, we all met for the shiva (the gathering of friends and family) at my cousin Barbara's beach house, which was a few blocks from the ocean and the perfect meeting spot for all of the guests and out-of-towners. We broke out pictures of my mom, ate delicious food, and told stories. Barbara's daughter serenaded us on her guitar with a few beautiful songs. It was truly touching.

Before the life ceremony on the beach, we had a minor graveside ceremony where my father was buried. Lisa, Sarah, and I were driving for what seemed like an hour to find this cemetery in Manalapan, New Jersey, to bury some of the ashes there; we planned to put the rest in the ocean.

Dad and Mom together again

We followed our directions and did find a cemetery, but it turned out to be the wrong one.

Someone said, "There is another cemetery over that way ..."

We drove another 10 minutes or so and were within a mile of the cemetery but didn't realize it. We finally got to the cemetery and remembered we had to go looking for the Hirshorne family plot. Lo and behold, we discovered a rather large, flat stone about 18" long in the shape of (ironically?) the State of New Jersey. This stone was laying right on the plot where my father was interred. Why? We don't know. It was just laying there, waiting to be discovered. Was the fact that we needed some sort of marker for my mom, and that it just "happened" to be the right size, right next to my father's gravestone, a coincidence?

This was an Orthodox cemetery, mind you. You don't go in there with a shovel unless you intend to bury a (whole) body. If anyone knew that I intended to bury a cremated body, they would have buried *me* instead! But I had my shovel ready, in case we needed it. I didn't care. I wanted to bury my mother next to my father and, come Hell or high water, I was going to do it!

Sarah said, "Are you out of your *mind*? You can't go in there with a shovel. They'll behead you!"

It was a good point, and I kind of liked my head the way it was, so I left the shovel in the car, not really knowing what to do but just "go with it."

"Okay, guys. What are we going to do?"

Lisa and Sarah said, "Let it unfold. Let's just see what happens."

The stone was sitting on our father's plot, which was entirely covered in white gravel, with a small Japanese Maple tree right in the middle. There was a little patch of dirt about 3 inches in diameter—soft, powdery dirt, not sand, and so soft that I could take my hand and scoop it right up without any effort.

Lisa said, "Mom planned this. No doubt about it. She was planning it while we were driving around!"

As I scooped up the dirt with my hand and dumped in half of the ashes, I said the kaddish (a prayer of remembrance) for her. At that point, I covered over the spot with the stone that was left for us. We found another small stone and scratched out (as if it were a headstone) "Beverly S. Hirshorne, Rest in Peace." We kissed Grandpa Saul's, Grandma Bea's, and our father's headstones by kissing our fingers and then touching the headstones. Then we took a picture of all three of our hands while we gently touched Mom's tombstone.

A new adventure

After we did this, Sarah said, "Mom, we need to leave now. We need to go to the beach to have your life ceremony."

Immediately after my sister said that, I looked down and saw a single, perfectly formed, fan-like mollusk shell (15 or so miles from the ocean), sitting on the plot, about 3 feet from my mother's New Jersey-shaped stone. There was a slight pinkish color to it. If I had gone right instead of left, I would have missed it. I *was* going right, but instead I changed my mind and decided to go left for some reason. We both saw the shell. I looked at Sarah, she looked at me, and we started laughing and crying at the same time! I still have that shell. It was actually used to hold a bit of my mother's ashes during the life ceremony on the beach in Belmar.

Seashell found on my father's plot

Just before Lisa flew in from Arizona for the funeral, she was given a crystal from a friend of hers. She loves crystals, so it had spiritual meaning for her. Somewhere along the line, she lost the crystal but mentioned many times later how sad she was that she lost it.

As we were walking back to the car from the gravesite, Lisa looked down and saw a strange-looking rock that had the letters "ILY" inscribed in it with a heart. "ILY" clearly meant "I Love You." The rock was lying in the parking lot of the cemetery immediately next to my car. Lisa had gone to the opposite side than Sarah and I had, and she was the first to see the rock. At this point, all three of us were speechless, and the ride back home was, well … very interesting.

Rock found next to my car in the parking lot

I tell this story to people and, of course, some are skeptical: "Someone bought it at the store and dropped it or put it there."

Really?

The cemetery was 15 or so miles from the beach. How did that perfectly formed shell get there? To suddenly just appear while we were talking about the beach? Plus the little pile of dirt? The headstone shaped like New Jersey? Each event could very well have occurred by "coincidence" separately, but the fact that they appeared in that order, on that day, and at that exact time? How do you explain that? To me, it reveals something that humankind has noticed for thousands of years: There is a strong connection between the spirit world and this one, which becomes more acutely evident around the time of the passing of a loved one. These moments are good to remember, as they can affect our everyday view of reality as well. Things *really* are not as they seem. This is so because of an *allegiance* to the physical dimension while we are in physical form.

At this point, we went to the beach for the life ceremony. The weather could not have been nicer or calmer. Well-wishers gathered around us in a circle, and we made our statements. People asked us if we could do their ceremony when they died. No one was sad; instead, they felt uplifted, warm.

I put the ashes in the mollusk shell. Sarah, Lisa, and I walked into the ocean, and I let the ashes wash away. Mom loved Belmar; she loved the ocean. All she ever talked about was Belmar. "I love my sweet Belmar! I love it!"

I once said, "Mom, for your final wish, I am going to give you Belmar!" Of course, I had to keep my promise. As I let her ashes flow into the ocean, I thought, "Mom, you are going to become one with the ocean."

She didn't have the guilt anymore, the discouragement. She was not a materialist. It didn't bother her that she had money one day and none the next. It didn't bother her that people judged her. She was the epitome of love, and all she did was give it. She didn't expect it back either. She was just so loving to her kids, to her family, and never complained about her situation in life. I really believe that we pick our parents, and I picked mine to learn a lesson about unconditional love. She showed me and everyone around her what unconditional love really is: devoid of guilt or any other condition. It is simply giving of your whole self, no matter what your "outside" circumstances reflect.

Unfortunately, this woman was judged for most of her life for either doing things differently than many of us do them or for not doing the things that many of us do. Imagine being 22 years old and blamed for your brother-in-law's death—just because you made a phone call to ask for help!

Some people might respond by falling asleep in life and becoming less alive than they could be; others might use the event as a catalyst to change their lives and awaken to the possibilities that lie hidden just beyond "normal" reality. In my family, the contrast between these two choices was stark. The self-destruction that occurred in a chain reaction, following Uncle Barry's death, is a phenomenon that could be studied under a philosophical or psychological microscope. It's the untold story of many families that suffer in silence, unable to wrap their minds around the slow-motion, emotional explosion inside them and put it into words.

At the same time, my siblings and I said, "Okay. This is really happening. We need to take care of ourselves, and take a different path."

I became determined (to the point of being obsessed) and decided that I was going to wake up and take responsibility for myself physically, emotionally, and spiritually. I would allow this pain to become a catalyst for complete transformation."

This "life thing" is a process of waking up from the slumber that we're all engaging in without even realizing it. We're asleep at the wheel, letting our subconscious mind—filled with paradigms and beliefs from our well-meaning parents, teachers, friends, and society as a whole—plan and carry out the entire trip. Although your subconscious mind is much more powerful than the conscious mind, it's the conscious mind that downloads the program *into* the subconscious. In other words, your outside circumstances do not *have* to dictate your response to those circumstances. None of us have to run on autopilot.

For example, many of us think that we have to "die" in order to experience what life is like on the "other side," the one that lies just behind the scenes. Who says so? We are simply programmed to believe this to be true. Many people around the world do not accept this notion and have a completely different paradigm when it comes to this subject. If you keep an open mind, you can change the way you look at (perceive) things.

As the late Wayne Dyer would say, "When you change the way you look at things, the things you look at change." Based on this premise, there are multiple ways to change your paradigm and see life through a completely different set of "eyes." Just a few of these may be things such as meditation, contemplation, alternative healing techniques, and music. How about tree-hugging? My point is that much of it comes down to what you believe will work *for you.*

At my mother's life ceremony, all kinds of strange things happened at the same time. Were they all just "coincidental"? Meaningless events clustered together for no apparent reason? Or is it possible that her spirit was in fact trying to communicate with us? One cannot reasonably discount the fact that there were nine or 10 different, unusual events, all of which seem to be associated with my mother's dying wish to have her ashes disposed of respectfully and meaningfully. The only "scientific" explanation one can offer is that someone went and bought the heart-shaped rock and carved the initials "I," "L," and "Y." Then, the mollusk shell, the powdery dirt, and the stone shaped like Jersey were bought, then left at key locations (one of which was right next to my car while we were in the cemetery)—all in the interest of trying to trick us. Really? What kind of person would *do* that? For that matter, who would have the audacity to do such a thing at a ceremony as solemn as a funeral?

The House That Jack Built

I f it isn't clear by now, this story is about shame and grief, and how we can either heal those wounds together or let them destroy us in solitude. Families are complex organisms—both spiritually and emotionally—and a single incident may trigger a chain reaction of destructive

I am now aware that the pain of that loss caused me to dig deep into spirituality and maybe, even unknowingly, metaphysics.

behavior that can cripple everyone in the family. That same incident could also become a turning point for everyone to come together and work as a team spiritually, if they so choose.

For some members of our family, the long-buried memories of Barry's death continued to be a source of toxic shame and remorse that led to a sense of denial, self-hate, and ultimately spiritual sleep. For others, this tragedy, though long forgotten and pushed into the recesses of the subconscious, became a reason to ask deeper questions about the meaning of life than most of us ever ask. I am now aware that the pain of that loss caused me to dig deep into spirituality and maybe, even unknowingly, metaphysics. I did this with the intention of trying to stop the pain with a dose of understanding of what it meant to be "alive" and what it meant to be "dead."

An English poem called "This Is the House That Jack Built" (written in 1755) expresses the kind of emotional and spiritual chain reaction that can happen at any time. I think you will see a few parallels to my story.

This Is the House That Jack Built

This is the house that Jack built.
This is the malt that lay in the house that Jack built.
This is the rat that ate the malt
That lay in the house that Jack built.
This is the cat that killed the rat
That ate the malt that lay in the house that Jack built.

This is the dog that worried the cat
That killed the rat that ate the malt
That lay in the house that Jack built.
This is the cow with the crumpled horn
That tossed the dog that worried the cat
That killed the rat that ate the malt
That lay in the house that Jack built.

This is the maiden all forlorn
That milked the cow with the crumpled horn
That tossed the dog that worried the cat
That killed the rat that ate the malt
That lay in the house that Jack built.

This is the man all tattered and torn
That kissed the maiden all forlorn
That milked the cow with the crumpled horn
That tossed the dog that worried the cat
That killed the rat that ate the malt
That lay in the house that Jack built.

This is the judge all shaven and shorn
That married the man all tattered and torn
That kissed the maiden all forlorn
That milked the cow with the crumpled horn
That tossed the dog that worried the cat
That killed the rat that ate the malt
That lay in the house that Jack built.

This is the rooster that crowed in the morn
That woke the judge all shaven and shorn
That married the man all tattered and torn
That kissed the maiden all forlorn
That milked the cow with the crumpled horn

TAKING A CHANCE ON LIFE

That tossed the dog that worried the cat
That killed the rat that ate the malt
That lay in the house that Jack built.

This is the farmer sowing his corn
That kept the rooster that crowed in the morn
That woke the judge all shaven and shorn
That married the man all tattered and torn
That kissed the maiden all forlorn
That milked the cow with the crumpled horn
That tossed the dog that worried the cat
That killed the rat that ate the malt
That lay in the house that Jack built.

This is the horse and the hound and the horn
That belonged to the farmer sowing his corn
That kept the rooster that crowed in the morn
That woke the judge all shaven and shorn
That married the man all tattered and torn
That kissed the maiden all forlorn
That milked the cow with the crumpled horn
That tossed the dog that worried the cat
That killed the rat that ate the malt
That lay in the house that Jack built.

Perhaps you can imagine the cow with the crumpled horn as the car that hit Uncle Barry, honking for him to get out of the way and ending up with a crumpled front end. Then imagine Barry as the family dog in the story, the one run over by a car, the one the car sent flying. Then picture Grandma Bea as the cat, so worried about who should be blamed for Barry's death that she called my mother the rat, just to have someone to pounce on.

My sensitive and open-hearted mother ate that poison pill of terribly misguided love, and began to believe that she somehow was that

80

rat. Her love was truly like malt, the love for our family that betrayed her, when it was pointed out that she was responsible for the death of her brother-in-law. As one tragedy led to another and another, this misguided love coupled with intense guilt (for something she had nothing to do with) ultimately destroyed her emotionally, spiritually, and finally physically. We all worked hard to turn that love around, and at times we almost accomplished it. Our objective was nothing short of getting our mother back to a healthy state—a spirit-led state, full of love for herself and others—but the pain was too much. It had quite literally become a habit from which she was doomed to never escape, and it completely engulfed every aspect of her life, until it ultimately led to her demise.

At the same time, my father, all tattered and torn, tried to love my mother, even as she continued to compulsively milk her own sense of shame and guilt about the car accident, swirling downward on her spiral of grief. Ultimately all of his attempts to cheer her up—and his boastful promises—fell short.

Then there's me, the scribe, who is looking at this long chain reaction of woe and writing it all down, trying to make sense out of it, trying like Hell not to be judgmental and just forgive, live, and *let* live. In fact, I am all shaven and shorn, striving to come clean about this chaos that was "in my face" the whole time I was learning to be a man. It's a big challenge to sort it all out, the whole intergenerational pattern of self-abuse and self-destruction, while still being a part of this unfolding story.

I imagine myself standing inside that house (the house of my life), my subconscious, and most of all the house of my heart, with all its broken windows. In order to learn how spirit really works, I turn to teachers, heralds of the dawn, roosters: Neale Donald Walsch, the late Wayne Dyer, Eckhart Tolle, Gregg Braden (see "Helpful Resources" on page 159), and many others. It could also be Kabbalah, the Old Testament, the New Testament, Bhagavad Gita, Quran, Tao Te Ching, or other scripture. Whatever philosophical approach or text you follow is irrelevant, as long as you resonate with its teachings.

The problems we see happening all over the world occur when we see ourselves as separate from divinity, each other, and everything "else." In other words, when particular religious, philosophical, or subjective ideas or points of view are thought to be the "only truth," that point of view is forced upon others—sometimes to the degree that the end result is violence and/or death. Do not do what works *best*. Do what works best for *you*! In the greater scheme of things, this idea will also turn out to be what works best for the "other."

Who then is the farmer who takes care of that enlightened rooster? It is The Big Guy—God—who watches over us all. The rooster knows that the farmer loves him and will always take care of him. Every time he crows, it's partly to share that love with the whole world. The rooster's call is heard for miles, telling us to "wake up!" There isn't just one rooster; there are hundreds of thousands of them all over the world, giving us the same message: "It's time to get moving, to start working to change this world and make it a better place to live!" We need to start by changing ourselves.

Some of these folks are famous and some not so well known—just as it should be. The divine farmer sows seeds far and wide, miracles of love and healing, offering learning experiences by the score for those who can recognize them as signs of hope, not hardship. Some seeds fall on barren soil, but a few seeds fall on fertile soil, and that's all it takes. Those seeds will bear fruit, and each fruit will leave behind a hundred seeds.

The horse is the Holy Spirit, the other side of God's divine nature, the ever-present essence of God that moves in what can *appear* to be mysterious ways. Perhaps the hound represents those who are faithful to God and who help God to do her work. The farmer's horn would be the divine word, which has existed from the beginning of time—the voice of God that speaks to us through our intuition, dreams, and meditations, urging us to live "on purpose," at a more consciously aware level than we are living.

The entire cast of characters I have mentioned in this book live in my "house," which is the house of my unconscious. Every event in the

**One truth I have learned is that our destinies are all interrelated,
and what affects one person affects us all.**

chain has become part of who I am as a person—emotionally and spiritually. Whether or not I created these events somehow is a good question. What is more important is how I react to those events and how I play out this hand that life has handed me. I choose to use each pang of heartbreak as a moment of truth to spur me on to greater and greater moments.

One truth I have learned is that our destinies are all interrelated, and what affects one person affects us all. The poem "This Is the House That Jack Built" teaches us that even a small incident, such as a rat eating some malt, can have global effects over a long period of time. We are all related through a divine connection—literally, not just metaphorically. We should strive to see each other as one in spirit, and try to take better care of each other.

The House of My Life

In January 2012, I had a dream that freaked me out a bit. It was deep, and I remember it affected me so much that I wrote it down as soon as I woke up. In my dream, a dark figure was climbing up the steps towards my bedroom where my wife and I were sleeping. We were in the Jersey shore house in which I grew up with my sisters some many years earlier. I started screaming at the figure while running towards it with the intent of destroying it. I woke up screaming into the darkness of the still, wee hours of the morning. Awake, I seemed to sense that I was still in that childhood house and could not shake the feeling for about 20 minutes. It was as if I were still dreaming but in a conscious state. I think the figure I confronted was myself—the Self I was trying to transcend.

WE are the only ones responsible for creating our realities. We are always at a point of choosing whether we want to be the *cause* of what

Why can't we describe Creation in the blink of an eye and, at the same time, describe evolution as expressing itself over billions of years?

happens to us or the *effect* of it. Most people take their cues from everyone and everything around them, but the answer is inside; it has always been inside. In one respect, I see this series of unending occurrences we call "life" as random events; at the same time, I see a parallel.

How do I react (or not react) to each of these events? What can I pick up from them? What is the lesson that can stand separately from itself?

Once again, in *Conversations with God*, Neale Donald Walsch elaborates, "I don't want to give credence to the this, or the that."

As human beings, we tend to look at things in black and white. It has to be this way or that way.

Walsch goes on to say, "Why can't it be both ways?"

Why can't we describe Creation in the blink of an eye and, at the same time, describe evolution as expressing itself over billions of years? The duality, which incorporates (in essence, which *is*) so much a part of who we are in this world of the relative (hot/cold, down/up, left/right), is constantly begging for answers. What's so bad about just *letting it be*? One day, we will all find out anyway.

I love the fact that such an amazing chain of events was required to get me to write this book and relay this message—one that I believe to be very necessary and important. Many have tried to tell their life story as a teaching tale, with varying levels of success. I want this story to be something different. I am not claiming to be *anything*. I don't need credentials to write my life story. All I am saying is that there is another way we can do things and see things. My life, as I have lived it, contains clues as to why we can seek better ways and how we might find them.

You can take away whatever you want from this tale (like the poem, "This Is the House That Jack Built"). I will not take offense. I have learned that whatever we experience with our senses—sight, smell, hearing, taste, and touch—is not necessarily the end-all to our experience, not by a long shot. If you compare the spectrum of light (e.g., ultraviolet, gamma, X-rays, radio waves, and microwaves) to what your eyes actually see, it would be like comparing the thickness of a dime to the Sears tower. Similarly, your senses tell you that you are stationary when in essence you are being rotated by virtue of Earth's spin on its axis at more than 1,000 mph, hurtling through space in an orbit around the sun at an average of 67,000 mph! With an open mind, you will see (but maybe not necessarily with your eyes) things that you may have walked right past in the "past." (Pardon the pun.)

The sequence of events that unfolded, eventually leading to the creation of this book, has created a compelling storyline that makes sense to tell. Like the poem, "This Is the House That Jack Built, "this" had to happen in order for "that" to occur, and "this" is going to happen down the line. For this reason, I don't believe in coincidence—*ever*. I don't even like the word. I prefer to see things as happening because of cause and effect, with events and occurrences that happen through both conscious and subconscious effort. In other words, at some level we attract them. Although this may be hard to "swallow" for many of us, more and more evidence is being revealed in the quantum physics and quantum mechanics fields, which scientifically explains this theory beyond the shadow of a doubt.

"Coincidence" is defined as a remarkable concurrence of events or circumstances without apparent connection. Based on this definition, the sequence in which these events occurred is irrelevant. The question would then be, "Are there reasons why they happened in that particular sequence?" Based on what you have read thus far, one would have to conclude "yes." On the other hand, referring to a quote on heaveniswithin.net, one still may be skeptical.

The quote goes on to say, "One can always find evidence to prove their particular theory about the way things are. If I am against that theory, I will find evidence to the contrary." The word "coincidence" implies by its very nature that there is no meaning, no cause and effect, and therefore no teaching. How do I process this? From an Ego perspective or from a soul's perspective? For instance, certain people will call a particular color "white" when the vast majority of others will see

We are cocreators with our Creator, a part of this beautiful mosaic known as "life."

the color as "black," and this author can't do a damn thing about that! My job is not to convince you of anything in particular but to allow you to see that not everything is black and white.

The Dark Side of the House

Perhaps the "House that Jack Built" represents the dark side of my story. However, this so-called tragic sequence of events was necessary in order to bring me to this point in my life, at this time, as well as to the realization that I am not just a biological "thing" or even an emotional Jack in the Box. Could it very well be then that there really is no such thing as a "dark" side?

I am a body/mind/spirit triune—forever in a state of unfolding and evolving in this eternal moment of now. We *all* are. We chose our palettes and paint before we arrived; we did not, however, choose what kind of picture to paint. This (hopefully) inspiring story, which started in 1962 and continues today, is in fact just the beginning. It is my very own painting, and it continues to change with (literally) every thought I have. It is a reflection of an eternal process of birth and rebirth, where we all decide what kind of picture we are going to create—and then create again.

We are cocreators with our Creator, a part of this beautiful mosaic known as "life." We are the "sum of its parts" but intuitively know that the whole is greater than the sum of those parts. At each point in the story—*all* of our stories—we have the option to react in one way or another, and we do so based on how well we can balance our Ego's perspective with our soul's perspective. Can we "react" to our life circumstances based on our understanding of life-affirming, spiritual principles, or are we going to choose to react in self-defeating, defensive, or destructive ways? The choice is, and will forever be, ours to make.

86

If we explore this "dark" side, which we each seem to experience mostly without exception, we need to ask the question, "Is it truly dark if it causes us to find within ourselves a wisdom that comes from absolute light?" Yes, the depression that my father and Grandpa Saul experienced for so many years must have felt dark and "heavy," but look at the revelations they had about spirit just before they passed over. I believe that, in the end, they were able to enter into the light as they "transformed" their physical selves rather effortlessly.

As I think about my next project, I see myself writing about finding the light switch, even when we're surrounded by darkness. This light switch may be within arm's length, but we keep walking right past it because we only have a tiny candle to illuminate our path. When we finally do flip the switch (with most of us waiting until we die to do so), we discover treasures that we could not perceive with the limitations of our five senses but that were waiting for us to discover all along.

You can transform the "perceived" darkness inside of you with the fact that the contrast is just doing its job by bringing you to clarity about whatever situation you are experiencing. When your consciousness opens up, your actual perception of light naturally changes. When your consciousness shuts down, or you choose to suppress the Self in favor of the Ego, you make a decision to experience that "darkness" as your reality, within varying degrees. Since we live in a world of duality, we need contrast in order to understand values. If we didn't first experience light, we wouldn't know what darkness felt like. As stated in *Conversations with God*, however, we don't need them next to each other in order for the contrast to make sense. At some point, we've experienced it all, *over many lifetimes,* and in the infinite universe, including both the physical and metaphysical realms. We may have even experienced intense darkness, but just not in the physical body we are now occupying. *We have driven down this road before and are well aware of the many potholes that lay before us. We now choose to take a different road.*

We will one day get to a point where we look at what we've created and simply ask, "Does what I have done (or maybe what I'm about to do) up until this point *serve me or not?*"

You have the option of reacting to that darkness, but you can also see it another way: It happened for a reason.

"Yes, I'm human, and I'm going to react at times—maybe to things that are causing me heartache or to things that I believe are missing in my life. I'm going to have a good cry and get it out. Then, I'm going to be thankful for what I *do* have, including the experience of knowing what I *don't* want." At this point, it becomes easier to manifest what we *do* want.

I'm going to ask, "How can I learn from this? What can I grasp? How can I make my life better?" When we are thankful for the things that do give us pleasure and concentrate on those things (however sparse they may be), they tend to increase in magnitude and quantity.

I experienced a lot of anxiety as a child as a reaction to these same events. I still carry that anxiety to some degree as a result of the subconscious downloads that still occur from time to time. On the other hand, I am so involved now with spirituality that those negative messages are constantly being erased and rewritten (through books, CDs, etc.) with new data, which provide a wonderful, new way of living, of creating reality as *I choose* to create it.

Gambler's Anonymous

S tarted in 1957 by two men who decided that they could not control their gambling, Gambler's Anonymous has helped millions of men and women who find themselves in the same predicament. Not only do they offer help for those whose lives have been completely taken over by gambling, but the group (now often called "G/A") has published many books and various articles filled with sturdy and helpful philosophical insights that can help nonaddicts as well. My father's addiction didn't get out of control until about 1968. At that point he

**I am so involved now with spirituality that those negative
messages are constantly being erased and rewritten.**

knew that, if he didn't do something quickly, he would lose Saul's (the stationery store started by his father) and his entire family.

After an initial family "intervention" on the part of Grandpa Saul, Grandma Bea, my mother, and a G/A representative, Dad conceded that he needed help and went to meetings on a regular basis. He got the help he needed and moved his way up the leadership ranks within the organization, helping others as he had been helped.

I went to some of those meetings, and they always started the same way: with a prayer that became the mantra of our family. It expressed in a few words the underlying principle that my parents tried to convey to me and my siblings our entire lives:

Serenity Prayer
God, grant me the serenity to accept the things I cannot change,
Courage to change the things I can,
And wisdom to know the difference.

My mother had these words embroidered, and she hung it on our wall for all to see. It held a prominent place in our dining room for many years and found a place on the wall in the hospital room after Mom was diagnosed with Stage IV pancreatic cancer. Quite frankly, it was the last thing I remember packing just after Mom passed away.

G/A influenced our families and our lives in too many ways to calculate. My mother would sometimes get involved with Gam-Anon (therapy for others affected by gambling) and would even make "vacations" for us kids out of the conclaves that G/A would hold. One such conclave was held at the Playboy resort in the Pocono Mountains of Pennsylvania. It brought the family together for a memorable vacation and allowed an 11-year-old boy to get a "glimpse" at what this area of Pennsylvania was all about. (By the way, the Poconos weren't the only mountains I saw!) There were many friends who came and went as a result of G/A. Most of them stayed around for my dad's entire life. They

The program, like all 12-step programs, is based on coming to the realization that you do not have control over the addiction.

were his support team and would continue to be to this day if he were still alive.

G/A is now in more than 35 countries, with multiple offices in many of them. The United States alone has thousands of meeting sites located in practically every part of each state. Their international headquarters, located in Los Angeles, can be contacted by visiting gamblersanonymous.org. I have nothing but praise for this organization, as it literally saved my father's life some 45 years ago, and I would highly recommend it to anyone who believes that gambling has taken over their lives. The program, like all 12-step programs, is based on coming to the realization that you do not have control over the addiction. When you can finally admit this to yourself, you give it to God and allow the "miracles" to unfold—and they do, as soon as you take your chance on God instead of a bunch of cards.

OUR MIRACLE BOY

Luck or Destiny?

In April 2008, my son Jason turned three. It's hard to believe that he almost didn't make it at birth. As I mentioned, he was born with a heart condition (pulmonary atresia), which nevertheless did not stop him from surrounding all of us with his love and blessings from Heaven from day one. Jason spent his first 21 days on Earth in intensive care. Someday, perhaps, this wound in his heart will lift him up to surrender to spirit in a way that will make him very powerful in affirming life. I hope so.

News of his heart condition certainly wounded my own. I would talk to the doctors each day, and then walk down to the gardens outside the hospital and cry my eyes out. It was just too much. After all the broken hearts in our family, I somehow expected him to start with a clean slate and a healthy heart. That didn't happen.

Jennifer and I knew what had to be done and, although she was earning quite a bit more than I was, she decided to quit her job as a marketing manager and take care of Jason. After relying on her substantially higher income, I used up a pension, which took me 17 years to build, and would gladly do it all over again to save my son's life. Jennifer returned to the work force when Jason was eight months old. She started slowly, selling for Welcome Wagon, but at that point our debt had become enormous, and the compensation—a commission only—was nominal at best. At the same time, I received a disappointing job review that included the dreaded words, "Needs improvement," after 20 years of praise. I received a mere 2% raise, even though I did (practically) everything they asked of me. It was a tough time. We started experiencing friction in our relationship. The pain of the job world had reached our hearts, and it affected our spiritual life.

I wrote to Jennifer, "I sincerely apologize (for what I said), and I hope that we can come to terms with this temporary glitch by seeing it as temporary. I believe in you, and you need to do the same. Try to concentrate on rising above mediocrity. We cannot thrive by telling ourselves that we have to be 'realistic.' If Edison thought that way, I'd be writing this with a quill pen by firelight. Believe that you *can* rise above this, and you will. It's that simple.

"I've written down a scenario of how I would like to see our lives play out from here on, including a new personal development company that I have been thinking about for some time now. I am so confident in the power of visualization that I'd bet my life on that outcome. When you believe that strongly in something, it has no choice but to manifest itself into your reality. Please try to see the lesson in all of this. I love you and want nothing more than for us to be happy."

Lucky to Have Problems

Jennifer and I were warned about six weeks before Jason's birth that there would be "problems." In fact, he'd be lucky to *have* problems. A miracle. If he were born without a pulmonary artery, it would mean certain death, and death would wipe away our so-called "problems." They mentioned all kinds of crazy scenarios that could happen, some more serious than others. The minute I heard the news, my knees went limp, and I felt like I was about to pass out. Nonetheless, we prayed for life, not death.

After our son was born, he needed a series of procedures, the second of which was a type of angioplasty, performed at a hospital in Virginia. I remember quite vividly lying flat on my back on a chaise lounge at the Ronald McDonald house (next to the hospital) just after the operation. I was alone, and it was raining quite heavily. I hardly noticed and didn't care. As rain pelted my face, I calmly took note of the trees blowing and bending in the wind. *They stayed flexible.* It took me a number of years to realize the subtle undercurrent to the scene unfolding in front of me.

I looked up and uttered with indignance, "Why me? What did I ever do to deserve this?"

As one might expect, there was no audible answer—just the sound of the rain.

Our eight-year-old daughter Brianna came to visit Jason in intensive care with her grandmother (my mother). He had tubes coming out from every direction just after the surgical procedure on his heart was completed. One tube was inserted into his trachea. I assumed it was there to feed him or assist with his breathing.

Brianna took it all in stride, pointing to her newborn baby brother and saying with a smile that could light up a room, "Look, Mommy. I have a new baby brother!"

Jason tried to cry, but the tubes were preventing him from doing so. I looked at him with a mixture of despair and utter joy. It was a long 21 days in the hospital. After months of oxygen therapy and two injections of blood thinner each day, our little boy started improving. His eating (contrary to the doctor's opinion) was not only "normal" but even hearty! It seemed this way from infancy right through to childhood. He appeared to even be excelling academically, which was miraculous in and of itself, considering that his brain was without oxygen for a period of time immediately after birth. However, he started to reveal a lack of certain social skills. It was apparent that he had ADHD (attention deficit hyperactivity disorder) and was not only a bit precocious but defiant as well. We knew it would be challenging, but we were ecstatic nevertheless that things were progressing so well.

The Birth of a New Me

How would we handle Jason's situation and all of our debts to boot? I prayed for a miracle, and that miracle turned out to be inside me. It all started with the horrible news that my son was born with a hole in his heart. Because of Jason's heart, I was more determined than ever to heal my own and find the miraculous in every new day.

I began to listen to audio books as I drove to and from work: anything written by the late Wayne Dyer, *The Divine Matrix* (Gregg Braden), *Three Magic Words* (Uell S. Andersen), *Conversations with God* (Neale Donald Walsch), *The Power of Now* (Eckhart Tolle), *Way of the Peaceful Warrior* (Dan Millman), and many more. I became filled with a life-affirming energy, and it changed everything.

I reached adulthood dreaming of what it would be like to be financially independent and have the freedom to do things "my way" and not get caught up in the rat race that seems to suck so many of us down the "rabbit hole." Meanwhile, I was not dealing well with the likes of anger, worry, and impatience—things that poverty and circumstances perceived as "not going your way" can teach you how to deal with, if you pay attention. That's how I saw things until my son was born, but then I woke up. This kid is a master teacher, which is to say that he pushes my buttons a lot. My wife is also a master teacher. She pushes my buttons on occasion, and I sometimes respond with anger. Then, as sure as the sun does shine, when I exude a particular vibration, I get it back sooner or later, 100% of the time, in one form or another. We *all* will—and, until we learn this to be so, it will continue ad nauseam.

Here's a true scenario to illustrate how anger creates more of the same. I was reacting to a bad day at work, cursing as I left the office. I got to my car and the blasted key wouldn't turn! I hit unheard-of traffic on the way home, stretching bumper to bumper for a few miles. I walked through the door, and my wife was on the phone, trying to get us bus tickets to see a school my daughter applied to in New York City. As I approached Jennifer, bristling with questions, she was about to hit

94

the "enter" button to seal the deal, and the computer screen froze! It unfroze a minute or two later, and the price of the ticket jumped $35! At that point, we were both pretty perturbed. I pursed my lips, closed my eyes, and walked into the family room to cool down.

This was a learning process. There were moments, especially in the beginning, when I was angry with God for offering me a son with an imperfect heart. Who was I kidding? Like *my* heart was perfect? I had just as much reason to be grateful for the fact that my son was *alive*—a living, breathing miracle.

Nowadays, I don't get angry about this situation. I am grateful for all the life lessons it has brought, especially about handling anger. They say you can't afford the luxury of an angry thought. Well, that's certainly true for me. Once you start becoming consciously aware of how you're actually attracting these scenarios (instead of believing that they are befalling you), it all becomes painfully obvious, and you have your "ah-ha" moment.

I realize that this is easier said than done. However, if we pause even for a split second before reacting to the "zing" that someone just unleashed, you'll see what I mean. We never *have* to react to anything or anyone with anger. That is a choice that our Ego makes. When the choice is made from the higher Self, we are given the opportunity to change the outcome of our experience then and there.

Is the Law of Attraction a bunch of fool's gold and fairy dust? If you think in terms of the law of *vibration*, it's really quite simple. When you emit a certain *frequency*, it attracts that exact frequency back. This may happen immediately or, in many cases, minutes, hours, days, or even months later. At this point, it may seem as though you are the "victim" of unwanted circumstances; in reality, you are simply experiencing the "looking glass syndrome."

Indeed, *all* of your life experiences are simply reflections of your thoughts about them. Don't like what you are experiencing? Change your thoughts about it! There are countless examples of people who refused to allow themselves to be victims of their circumstances. Some of the more famous ones include Oprah Winfrey, Steve Jobs,

When approached with aggression, we think that we need to give aggression back.

Albert Einstein, Helen Keller, and Nikola Tesla. Others include Laird Hamilton, Liz Murray, Pete Carroll, and G. M. Rao (see "Helpful Resources" on page 159 for more information). None of these people allowed their circumstances to dictate their ultimate life experiences.

In physics, opposites attract; in metaphysics, like attracts like. In acoustical physics, we see it more clearly. With "sympathetic vibrations" or "entrainment," a vibrating string can make a nearby string respond and play the same note. That's how consciousness works. Everything is energy, which is frequency/vibration. When you vibrate with the frequency of anger, depression, anxiety, or fear, what do you think you will attract?

When approached with aggression, we think that we need to give aggression back. For example, we hear, "To fight terrorism, we need to eliminate the terrorists." How exactly are we supposed to "kill off" a paradigm that has buried itself deep into the psyche of a people? For that matter, how many terrorists need to be eliminated before we figure out that, for every two that we "remove from society," three take their place? Why don't the vast majority see this problem as systemic? We simply want it to go away but don't seem to realize that, in the immortal words of Albert Einstein, "We cannot solve a problem with the same mindset that created it."

Most of us seem to forget that the root of the problem is consciousness, and to rid ourselves of the problem (*any* problem, really) requires that we change our approach and our consciousness as a whole. How do we raise our consciousness to the point where we finally realize this? We start with the realization that it must begin with the Self. You can't always one-up the next guy. He's a part of you on some level. When you bang him over the head with a hammer, you are doing violence to yourself. Then he gets a bigger hammer, and on and on it goes!

My personal crisis, requiring a massive shift in consciousness, began with the birth of a beautiful, little boy born with a defective pulmonary valve in his heart.

At his birth, I thought, "It's over. What can we do? We don't have the resources to deal with this kind of thing!" It seemed horrible, but it was the greatest experience of my life and the impetus for this book. I was sitting in the rain, with raindrops pelting my face, looking up at God and crying, "Why did you *do* this?"

There was no response, as if to say, "You have to figure it out yourself."

So that's what I did.

As I previously mentioned, I started listening to Neale Donald Walsch's *Conversations with God*, and it completely changed my life. I must have listened to it 10 or 11 times, and it seemed to help make sense out of the crisis. It led me to some of the other sources of wisdom that have changed my life.

For the period of time that I was into the Kabbalah, it was very helpful, but I soon discovered that there was *no one direction* that I, nor anyone else for that matter, needed to go. I was gaining more and more knowledge about this stuff, and learning more and more about metaphysics. I realized that there was no *one* right path to God, Jesus, Allah, or Krishna. These labels don't define the *essence* of divinity. When you label something—*anything*—you have to be careful about defining it for others. How you "see" something may not be the same way your neighbor sees it. That doesn't make it wrong, just different. Want to go hug a tree? Go ahead and hug a tree if it "connects" you. What someone else thinks about *how* they connect is their business, not yours.

Brianna is into Judaism in a very religious, Orthodox way. I don't judge that because, for her, it works. Based on dialogue from *Conversations with God*, I have learned to look at the foundation of the home we are all building. This is the home that took our whole lives to build. If we see bricks that are chipped and broken (i.e., judge how others do things if it's not the way we do them), we should take those bricks out and replace them. It makes sense. I'm *not* of course suggesting that we demolish and then rebuild the entire structure. I am however saying that we look at the foundation; if it is in need of repair, change it.

When you tell this to someone who is steeped in dogma, they might say, "This is what the book says I have to do, so I have to do it, and I can't deviate." They won't be comfortable with this kind of advice, and that's just fine if it truly serves them.

That is the question we must constantly ask ourselves: "Does it serve me?"

If it doesn't resonate with you, should you do it? God is not going to care if you are Jewish and eat a cheeseburger. Ask, "Do *I* care?"

A number of us go through life with beliefs that we never question and which may not make *even close* to 100% sense. We believe that we have to do something according to some book. It's easier to take this book, read the rules in it, and say, "You know what? I don't have to think about this because it's all right here."

Many people don't *want* to think. They just want someone else to tell them when to do something, how to do it, and even *what* to think!

It's harder to say, "This rule I grew up with doesn't resonate with me anymore. It doesn't serve my soul or my soul's purpose."

Inside of all of us is the connection to our very source, to our Creator. That inside connection is the "I" that asks, "Do I care if I eat a cheeseburger?" It has all the answers to every question we could ever ask. It does not have to rely upon anything outside of *itself* to receive an answer, and all we have to do is to call upon it.

Let the Children Lead

Keeping Jason going every day, while trying to understand him and what he was going through, took up a lot of my wife's and my attention. We began to ignore Brianna's needs, and perhaps even some of our own. We were locked in combat mode from the day Jason was born, and it wasn't serving us any longer.

> **Whenever time was an issue, our lack of patience (often related to a failure to plan ahead realistically) gave rise to our children feeling inadequate and unfulfilled.**

Then we started to encounter rebellion from both children at once. I didn't know what to do. I meditated on this and came up with a surprising answer: They did not feel as if they were involved enough in our creative process as a family.

For example, when I tried to help him with his pants, shirt, hair, or washing, Jason constantly told me, "I can do it *myself*, Daddy!"

The look on his face after accomplishing the smallest of tasks was priceless. Brianna telegraphed a similar message. She wanted more autonomy. Whenever time was an issue, our lack of patience (often related to a failure to plan ahead realistically) gave rise to our children feeling inadequate and unfulfilled. They both longed to assert themselves as independent, creative partners at any price. They wanted what I wanted: to be a cocreator with the universe. The apples fall not too far from the tree! At times, Brianna would push my buttons just to garner attention. I'm sure she felt that Jason was getting most of the attention, which was true, and felt that attracting negative attention was the next best thing to positive attention, and much better than none at all.

Needless to say, things got pretty chaotic around the Hirshorne house until a solution was found. I resolved the issue by letting them both play a bigger role in the creation of their reality. As "God" says in *Conversations with God*, "We were put on this earth not so much to go through our lessons, or to discover who we are, but to create and to discover who we wish to *become* in any given moment."

We could have bribed them with treats, tickets to concerts, Facebook, cars, and anything else under the sun, but I don't think we'd have seen any tangible resolution until they felt like they had a hand in creating their own reality.

Jennifer was concerned about how we as parents would handle this big transition between ourselves and our offspring. I told her not to worry.

No day is ever perfect, and no day is so bad that it augurs the end of the world.

"When this transition occurs, as it must, and as they get older and take on more responsibility, you will have less to do with them and will most likely someday long for the days when you had a say over everything going on in their lives. You will be free of making lunches; keeping up with the incessant scheduling of practices, rehearsals, appointments, doctor visits, dentist visits, and meetings with teachers; laundry; schlepping to and fro; and making dinner to every picky eater's total satisfaction. They may not say it often, but they appreciate all you do for them. They long, however, to assert themselves and to be free to cocreate with their Creator. We do not own them; they belong to themselves. All we did was allow them to come through us."

God Is in Charge

The financial aspects of having a son with ongoing medical needs are too complex to explain here, and hopefully most readers will never need to know. They are challenging, but I never gave up taking a chance on life. On November 1, 2007, I decided to take a break from work and walk to the convenience store to check my lottery tickets from the previous two days.

During my meditative walk, I kept looking up and muttering, "Just give me a sign that the wait is finally over!"

To my disappointment, I just got a donut hole. Zero response!

Upon checking the tickets, I saw the same words on the now-familiar message screen: "NOT A WINNER!" I knew this wasn't true in the game of life; in this game, however, it unfortunately was. I started my long walk back to work a little dejected but still upbeat.

Just then, a car came out of nowhere with a bumper sticker that read, "Relax. God is in charge!"

As the car passed out of sight, I looked up and smiled in gratitude.

I took the word "relax" to heart and remembered to calm myself—a key to tuning in and listening to spirit.

A Healing from Within

There are no completely good or bad days. Nothing is ever black and white. No day is ever perfect, and no day is so bad that it augurs the end of the world. I learned this from raising a son with an imperfect heart in an imperfect world. Most days, there would be moments of struggle, so I had to decide whether to beat myself up or make each day as fun and uplifting as I knew how to do. Naturally, I chose the latter, and I encourage others to do the same.

At a few years old, Jason would never get out of the car without destroying it first—his signature gesture. One night, he grabbed Jennifer's glasses and threw them under the seat. We didn't know. We looked all through the house and all through the car, except between Brianna's feet. She never once said, "I will help you find them, Mommy." She just sat and stared into thin air during the whole drama. Finally, she got out of the car, and we found the glasses in front of her on the floor, under the front seat.

This is how things were for a long time. We, just like Jason, were all learning to cope with inconvenience on a grand scale.

I was driving home one day soon after that and decided that I would let God handle the details. I was determined not to sweat the "small" stuff and just concentrate on the big picture. Just then, a white van with a license plate that read "MKDREAM" suddenly appeared out of nowhere and pulled in front of me.

I thought of Reverend Dr. Martin Luther King, Jr., his impossible dream, and the impossible odds he had against him. Many of his predecessors had been killed trying to do what he wanted to do, but he had a dream and a plan of how to do things differently. Part of his plan was to talk to God every day and look for signs. Even as he was accepting the Nobel Peace Prize, there were threats to his life, and obstacles that would have caused many brave men and women to back down and hide. All I had to fear was a bunch of credit cards.

Suddenly I felt that my life had turned a corner and the good stuff was directly ahead. I felt "plugged in," with no other way to describe it. After that, I began to notice that the sunsets were becoming more and more spectacular each day. Was it me or the sky? Was it God opening my eyes to the wonderful beauty of life around me? Life suddenly felt like it was supposed to feel, and it was good to be alive.

It also hit me hard because my first two initials are MK. Yes, I do think sometimes that God has a ripping sense of humor. She likes to show me once in a while that she does love me and has taken the trouble to have the universe personally monogrammed for me, like a pair of cheesy cuff links. If you quiet your mind enough, and consciously direct it to look for the "signs," you will begin to see them as well. Apparently, anyone and everyone can tap into this at times, often when our feet are most deeply in the fire, and even when we are not "under the gun" but simply open to the experience. I can't explain it scientifically, but it certainly cheered me and lifted my spirit that day.

I will never forget the day I hit bottom and wisely went to see a good therapist for a "checkup from the neck up."

She asked, "On a scale of 0 to 10, with 10 being the most stress and angst you can imagine, where are you right now?"

Of course, I said, "Eleven!"

After something similar to eye movement desensitization and reprocessing (rapid eye movement while following lights), I was down to about a seven out of 10. I prayed that this feeling of dread would finally leave and never return, as our financial situation was a bit on the challenging side—from constantly borrowing against credit cards while our income dwindled away.

If you quiet your mind enough, and consciously direct it to look for the "signs," you will begin to see them as well.

It had been three years since our son's birth and, although he had recovered from his most serious illness, the economy itself seemed to be in "intensive care." All you kept hearing on the news was, "Worst unemployment numbers in years!" and "Dow drops another 500 points!" Those reports didn't do much to heal my already fragile heart. I was looking for a solution for these blues from both inside and outside of myself.

That night, Jennifer and I went on a walk with my beloved dog and looked up at the night sky, wondering if God really was aware of me, thinking of me in any way, or hearing my side of the conversation. The stars looked particularly bright, especially the "twins" constellation. I noticed a cloud formation that looked exactly like "I love you" in the American Sign Language for the deaf! I wanted to show Jennifer, but it vanished before I could get her attention.

The next morning, I awoke at 5 a.m. for a nice walk, vowing to transcend the feelings of dread that dogged my steps. While on my way to work, I was playing a CD by Andrea Bocelli, a great tenor who sings with a lot of heartfelt, angelic energy, and I experienced what could only be described as a "divine orgasm." I suddenly felt overwhelmed with an intense, pleasurable feeling, which was so sudden and powerful that it left me sobbing and breathless. I had to shut off the music to compose myself before I had a car accident. I was so tearful that I needed to take time to get myself together before arriving at work.

Upon walking into the building, I greeted my boss with a cheerful, "Happy Friday, Paul!" My eyes were probably still red from sobbing.

He asked, "What's got you so down in the mouth?"

"Nothing," I responded. "Just the opposite, Paul. Just the opposite."

Some Miracles Rely on Us

The *Zohar* teaches us that, if you want to create a miracle, you have to go outside your comfort zone. In November 2008, Jennifer had just started working full time after three years of working on and off at a couple of part-time jobs and a few attempts at running her own business. We had dumped quite a bit of cash into her business ventures with very little to show for it. The bills did not stop coming in during that time period, and I had borrowed heavily against the credit cards to stay afloat and pay the mortgage. We were buried up to our necks in debt, and the tide continued to rise. If we didn't do something soon, it would spell financial ruin for sure. Our combined incomes exceeded the national average for family income; yet, as impossible at it might seem, I worried that our expenses would exceed our income.

I went into work one day, and an associate told me a story about her friend. This woman had just gotten a divorce, lost her home in a foreclosure, and was about to get kicked out of a rented townhouse. My associate said that the woman's daughter was being made fun of at school for wearing old, worn-out clothes and was teased by the other children to the point of torture, like a scene from *Lord of the Flies*. The other children even destroyed this poor girl's glasses while she was riding the bus home.

Upon hearing this, I was so moved that I went out at lunchtime to buy a Thanksgiving card. Then, feeling that it was not enough, I wrote in it a favorite quote "Better to light a candle than to curse the darkness." Still feeling that it wasn't enough, I inserted $50 into the card. As I did, I closed my eyes, held my breath, and said a prayer for us both.

I sealed the card and gave it to my associate, asking her to give it to her suffering friend. There will always be people who are worse off than we are. If I needed a miracle in my life, I was certain that this poor, single mother needed one more than I did.

We are constantly being tested, and I was not about to fail this test. When we are finally able to subdue our Egos, the spiritual side is free to scale the heights of Heaven. My associate and her husband were so moved by this gesture that they surprised *me* some two weeks later with a $75 gift card to a favorite local restaurant. I even took a day off of work to enjoy some downtime. It was the best lunch I ever had!

My Last Dollar

I was down to one, last, faded dollar in my aging wallet, and I spent it on a cookie that I got out of a vending machine at work. That machine was not unlike the workplace where it stood, the job to which I had just given over 20 years of my life, dumping out paychecks into my hands in order to keep me from starving. After that dubious investment in my future, I was walking around with a total of seven cents to my name. With a balance of around $18 in my check register (even though I padded the account with a few hundred unrecorded dollars), a mortgage that was "underwater," a hundred or so in savings, and two days' countdown to payday, I had to hang on. Did I mention that my credit cards were maxed out? Of course, you guessed that.

The bills were starting to mount at a faster and faster pace along with the pressure to get them paid. I simply had to do something and fast. I tried to calm myself down and meditated for a bit, thinking that a calm mind might bring me an answer. In any case, it sure beat worrying about it.

I went out to get some milk at the Giant grocery store, which was within walking distance, and I figured that the walk would do me good. As I entered the store, I noticed a sign that had not been there two days earlier: "Help Wanted." *Mmm* ... maybe this was the answer I was looking for. The customer service clerk handed me an application and, within two weeks, I started my "night" job as a cashier. It wasn't a ton of money, but it was a start.

Ideas started to flow about how to consolidate my debt. Amazing what a clear mind and a little extra help (in the way of dead presidents) can do for the psyche! I decided to seek out the advice of an attorney

Sometimes when we're looking for a door to open, a window opens instead.

friend in case I needed Chapter 13 bankrupcy filing. After a cash-flow statement had been drafted and a few "tweaks," a budget was put into place. We had worked out a game plan that didn't require such drastic measures as a Chapter 13 filing. Whew! I was even able to refinance our mortgage under the new government bailout program for homeowners. I knew that it would be some time before I was "out of the woods," but, for the time being, I was making progress.

About eight months later, as tax time approached, I was starting to get a bit nervous. Would I receive a tax refund as I did the previous year? Would I owe? The latter possibility did not give me too many warm and fuzzy feelings. I went to see my accountant a bit forlorn (gee, *that's* hard to understand!) and got ready to file in the same way a frightened child faces a vaccination at the doctor.

"Well," she said, "you're definitely not getting the same amount as last year."

My heart sank into despair. I braced myself for the bad news.

She laughed. "You're getting *twice* as much!"

I couldn't move my lips for a second. That much money could hold back the creditors, at least for a little while, and maybe even allow me to cut back on my hours at the Giant. Maybe I could quit! Was this the miracle I needed? Let's just say that things were at least moving in the right direction. Sometimes when we're looking for a door to open, a window opens instead. Hey, at least I could breathe in that nice, fresh air. I took a chance on life, and guess what? I'm still here.

The Bird of Freedom

stepped into Starbucks to grab some tea to go with my brown-bag lunch. A bird casually flew in while the door was still open. The bird started panicking and smashing into windows. You'd think some of these Bethesda [Maryland] businessmen and women would have helped the poor bird, but *no*! One guy rolled up his *Wall Street Journal* and actually started swatting at the bird! Another woman tried to stomp on it.

"The bird was flat on the floor. It looked right at me in distress; it was as if the bird were sending me a mental message: 'Please, help me!'

"Then, with an angry burst, I snapped at the dude who was trying to hit the bird with his *WSJ*: 'Stop!' I opened the door, and let the breeze waft in. The bird got up, slowly walked towards the door, lifted his wings, and flew away. True story!"

This is not my story, and I was not there, but my friend Dan was. I believe it happened. I also believe that he was meant to be at Starbucks at that moment to free the bird from suffering. Everyone involved had a part to play. If they didn't play *their* parts, Dan could not have played *his*. Everyone had something to learn from it.

Birds are often associated with the soul or with spirit. Medieval paintings show spirit birds leaving the bodies of dying men as an expression of the soul's departure. If this were a dream, we would probably suggest that the bird was the expression of the spirit of God in this world. Holy people try to maintain this spirit of freedom and innocence as they go about their day.

The people in Starbucks were faced with a sign that the creative, childlike inner spirit was trapped inside the confines of their worldly success, and their spirit was suffering. This untamed nature still fluttering inside struck them as a threat to their sense of control and safety, and they sought to destroy it in order to stop the suffering and kill the pain.

Danny, the hero of the tale, saw the beauty of the spiritual life in the bird and tried to free it, perhaps as a way of freeing himself, his own spirit. Some would see the doorway as a symbol of the opening of the heart, some as an opening of the mind, and others as a symbol of the third eye—the doorway to the soul. The *Wall Street Journal*, although in real life a fairly open-minded publication, represents in "dream time"

> To quote the late, great Wayne Dyer from the convention, I "will not die while the music is still playing in me." Life is good.

the wall of containment and control that office work tends to foster, so that more work can happen and that we all "get it done."

In other words, the long-standing rules of conduct that are supposed to make business cubicles (four walls) safe and productive were being used as a weapon to destroy the spirit within us, and Danny the Hero put a stop to it. The businesspeople were symbolic of all those controlling forces of commerce that try to stamp out nonconformity, spontaneity, and creativity for reasons that are sometimes hard to understand. Spirit spoke to Danny, as it does to us all. In this story, only Danny heard, and he acted. He freed his spirit and made sure that the others knew how to do the same, opening the doors to new, unimagined possibilities.

The Promise We All Should Make

I attended a heart-stirring authors' convention around March 2013: Hay House's "I Can Do It" seminar held at the San Diego Convention Center. After a few hours, I became so totally "juiced" from the positive energy of several thousand people converging in one spot that I could hardly contain myself! We were all hoping to learn how to transform our lives and careers into something incredible. Gregg Braden was inspiring, and the late Wayne Dyer was, as expected, at the top of his game. Christiane Northrup and Loretta LaRoche, on the other hand, had the 95% women in the audience in stitches while they poked fun at us guys. All I could do was smile and shake my head ruefully.

I went outside during a break, and I passed a homeless man about 100 feet from the convention center. I gave him a buck and kept on going, heading for a quick bite before my next seminar. The restaurant was packed, and I didn't have much time, but I decided that I would not let that deter me.

The hostess looked around and said, "Just one minute, sir." She came back after that minute, signaling "right this way."

While dining at this amazing restaurant and putting myself in the late Wayne Dyer's shoes, I imagined myself not just as Michael Hirshorne but as "Michael K. Hirshorne, published author." I thought of the homeless guy on the street and ordered a little "extra" (some cookies). After paying for my meal with a credit card, I noticed that my wallet had a few $20s in it but no smaller bills. For the life of me, I could not get the bartender's attention to break a bill, so I left.

The homeless man was still sitting in the same spot, as I hoped he would be. I placed the bag of fresh, homemade cookies at his side, looked directly into his forlorn and weathered face, and gently said, "If I give you this money, will you promise me something?"

He could barely get the words out. "Ye-e-ess, sir?"

"Will you promise me that you won't give up on yourself or on humanity, and will you believe and know that the world is still a good place to be?"

I received a polite nod and a "Thank you, brother!" It was probably more than he had ever received in his tattered hat from the combined offerings of literally hundreds of people who passed him. I headed back to the convention center with a rather large smile on my face. Yup, the world is still a good place to be!

I related this story to my mom, and we both became emotional. I promised her that I would not sit idly by while the world spun on its axis. To quote the late, great Wayne Dyer from the convention, I "will not die while the music is still playing in me." Life is good.

The Carpenter

I remained on my self-imposed, natural "high" for several weeks after the "I Can Do It" convention in San Diego. While at the office one day, about six weeks after the convention, I decided to use my lunch break to run some errands. On the way to the bank, I spotted a panhandler whom I had seen before. I got money from the bank and started walking back to work. This same panhandler started walking towards me and identified himself as the man I had given money to two weeks before. He said he was an out-of-work carpenter, living in a hotel with his two kids. (I thought of Jesus, a poor carpenter from Nazareth.)

As it turned out, just after I met him the last time, I was speaking to a buddy who used to work at my company and who now did carpentry and painting on the side and had more business than he could handle. I gave the panhandler a few dollars for lunch and my friend's phone number. He received a handout and a hand up.

Many people talk the talk, but it is more important to walk the walk. God does *not* work in mysterious ways. If we took more time listening and less time talking, we would hardly miss a cue. I was going to drive to the bank, but a certain something convinced me to walk, and I listened, thus making the connection I needed to make. I never saw that guy standing on the corner and panhandling for money again. I don't know if he did land some work with my buddy, but it really doesn't matter. He felt good that he was recognized as a human being with worth. I felt good *for* him. We both won.

Miracles and Money

Not long afterwards, my wife called me on her cell phone while I was shopping, and she was excited. We had been worrying about how to pay for Brianna's bat mitzvah and praying for help.

> **When I say that I "changed my attitude," I mean that I try very hard to think more about what I *do* want rather than about the *lack* of what I want to experience.**

I had even said to Jennifer, "I'm done worrying about money, honey. We're giving it over to 'the manager.'"

A prime opportunity for investing in a self-directed, individual retirement account (IRA) real-estate deal suddenly came about by way of an old friend. He was putting something together with four other partners, which required just about as much money as I had in my IRA account. I was previously getting around 2% on that money and decided to investigate. After running the numbers, it turned out that, if we held the property for eight or more years, we could all get close to 18% return on our investment. Does God rock or what? And who *was* that guy on the street corner?

There were many windfalls after that. A department store gave me $75 cash back on a pair of shoes my wife had bought years earlier, no questions asked. A $50 check from Hadassah (a Jewish women's organization) came in the mail at just the right time, along with other windfalls, some a bit bigger than $75. I even remember being "surprised" by a few unexpected checks that arrived in the mail. One day while I was busily working away at a spreadsheet, my boss motioned that he wanted to see me in his office. I of course expected a browbeating but, to my amazement, he shocked me with word that our company did better than expected. We would all be receiving a bonus in our next paycheck! All of this happened because I changed my *attitude* about money as well as anything else I chose to attract into my life.

When I say that I "changed my attitude," I mean that I try very hard to think more about what I *do* want rather than about the *lack* of what I want to experience. If there is any truth to the words, "Your thoughts (plus feelings) create your reality," I want to be certain to be thinking positive thoughts! There are no coincidences, only serendipitous events in time. The more we remove fear and doubt, the more room we make for our creations to come through unabated.

Some People Are Not Ready for a Miracle

I was taking my lunchtime walk and spotted what was obviously a homeless lady, about 20 yards ahead. My impulse was to hand her a few bucks as I walked past, but my mind started to justify why I should keep on walking. I kept going and ran an errand. On the way back, I spotted her again and questioned whether or not I should make contact. I got up the nerve to ask her if she was okay and if she had anything to eat that day. I expected her to say "no," which would be my cue to hand her some money and move on.

To my surprise, the woman said, "Yeah, I just ate!" At that point, she got defensive and paranoid, and then became angry. She looked at me funny and said, "Are you a Christian?"

"No."

She replied that John the Baptist told her about me and warned her that I would be coming to talk to her. I assumed at this point that she was mentally ill. She muttered more than a few expletives as I walked away.

I went back to work, thinking the whole time that I should have just given her the money when I first thought of it, no questions asked. I overheard an office mate telling her friend that she was short on cash. Aha! This was what the money was *really* for! I loaned her the few dollars that I put aside for the homeless lady. I also realized that a lesson was being revealed: Sometimes we need to reverse the usual thought-word-deed process. Sometimes we need to do the deed, so that we have a new thought about it before the mind jumps in and kills the thought, and in turn stops the deed. Thank you once again, Neale Donald Walsch! I learned not to judge people or take too much pity on folks who don't want to be pitied.

I learned not to judge people or take too much pity
on folks who don't want to be pitied.

A Change of Consciousness

The events and circumstances we are experiencing (that we refer to as "our lives") are always neutral in and of themselves. How we react to those events however is entirely up to us. The third week of November 2007 was somewhat frustrating for me. After returning to work from a vacation a bit late, I brought in chocolates for my coworkers. I hastily approached our lunchroom table, and I dropped the chocolates all over the floor while trying to open the package. After responding with a few "choice" ones, I went back to my desk.

Within five minutes, Jennifer called to tell me the news: Her car needed $1,000 worth of repairs. That afternoon, my cell phone broke, and that evening I dropped my electric razor into the toilet while trying to dump out the stubble. The fall broke the cartridge head, and I had to buy a new razor. Talk about a bad day!

At the same time, I was finding dimes all over the place, which seemed to be a message from spirit that life can change on a dime. A coworker bought me lunch for no particular reason. (I also got a notice in the mail that I had won $57,000, but that's another story. Those things seldom work out like we hope they will. Still, it was nice seeing that letter. Oh, well.)

Later, I went to the emergency room for what I thought was a stress/anxiety attack, with tingling in my hands and feet and a slight stomach ache. It wasn't such bad news: I was low on potassium. They gave me a pill, and I was soon back on track.

A spiritual teacher whom I regard highly—we'll call her Angel Ann—told me that there is much more to these types of feelings than meets the eye. They are familiar to those who journey frequently through inner planes of reality and to other levels of consciousness. We can have the same sort of experience that I was having from low potassium while being "out of body." Ringing and buzzing can be felt when we shift dimensions *out of* and sometimes back *into* the "physical." We simply need to surrender to it. Channelers and spiritual travelers often feel lightheaded, hot, cold, dizzy, spacey, and then clear.

The body is a huge antenna for energy, and the energy can be very strong. Sometimes we lie in bed and feel like we are spinning. The out-of-breath, spacey feeling can occur as we bring in more of our soul's vibration when the body is not yet accustomed to it, like running more charge through a wire than its rating allows. The stomach pains we feel may be fear of our own power. We don't always allow the process to be graceful—to breathe and relax. Instead, we may tense up when this new energy comes in. If we try to resist the process, it can even throw our bodies out of physical alignment. Of course, it's nothing a visit to the chiropractor can't fix!

Answers to Emptiness

There was a certain emptiness in the heart as I was growing up, which ran deep. It was an aspect of life that was ever present, and it pervaded my entire family although no one ever talked about it. Different people would react differently to it. It affected everyone, even myself as an infant.

In therapy, I tried to understand it. "Why am I so *anxious* all the time?" I could have thought, subconsciously, "It's all my fault." If I hadn't cried, Grandma Bea would never have made that fateful phone call, to say to Barry, "Please come over!"

As I mentioned earlier, I openly sobbed in the therapist's office because I could practically hear Uncle Barry in the afterlife, calling to me: "Michael! It's not your fault! It was meant to happen to me. It was something that my soul needed to have happen."

The visits to the therapist helped me sort out some things intellectually, but maybe this cathartic release was the most important step. I

~~~~~~
**Channelers and spiritual travelers often feel lightheaded,
hot, cold, dizzy, spacey, and then clear.**
~~~~~~

say this because, as my father's son, I grew up thinking, "If I just don't cry … if I just don't cry …"

Imagine being a young child and thinking that crying was so shameful! I had to keep it all inside. Did I think Dad would spend even less time with me if I showed emotion?

I suddenly recalled a memory I had about Grandma Shirley. She had a lot of sayings that would come up from time to time, such as, "Waste not, want not" and "Any damn fool can spend a dollar, but it takes a wise person to save it." The quote that came flooding back however was, "Don't cry, or I'll give you something to cry about!"

The beauty of going to a therapist is that you have permission to cry. In fact, in most cases, you are paying for the privilege, and it is worth it! It's a gamble that is likely to pay off—sometimes right away; sometimes later on—but it's a sure bet. Take my word for it!

Aftermath

I have had my share of stress in life, and yes, some of it has slipped by my awareness and taken the form of physical aches and pains. It's all relative. Without my connection to spirit, which is guiding me around one pitfall after another, both inwardly and outwardly, I can honestly say that I might be dead by now … but I am very much alive, and well, and living in joy.

I had a painful medical procedure years ago, after which they prescribed oxycodone for pain relief. The doctor didn't tell me that I had to *slowly* wean myself off this stuff; unfortunately, after 30 tablets, I just stopped. Withdrawal symptoms, similar to heroin withdrawal, can occur after only three days of taking this drug, and the effects apparently last for months. As is typical of my spirit-guided life, I found this out accidentally (as if there *are* any accidents!) by walking past a TV in our office building lobby. The show explained the side effects of painkillers in this class of drugs. I couldn't sleep for weeks because of this toxic panacea: anxiety, nervousness, panic attacks … you name it. Thankfully I am fine now.

Spiritual Healing

I booked a session with a spiritual healer. I didn't know what to expect but was wide open to receiving, well … pretty much *anything*. After the first five minutes passed, my body started to experience a kind of hum that went from my feet to my head, and it grew more intense. I soon felt as if I could almost rise up and out of my body. At that point, I had to open my eyes, tell myself to calm down, and just experience it. I concentrated on releasing the negative energy and began to feel both physically and spiritually whole. As I left the session, my headache made a last stand. I guess I stirred up the hornet's nest.

The next morning, I walked into my office with a renewed energy and sense of purpose. The headache was still there but much dissipated. From this point (I emphatically decided in my head), I would live every day with *intention* and let the universe figure out the "how."

Jason continues to thrive, and let me tell you that he is one smart kid! Aside from his mechanical and computer abilities, he seems to like acting (taking after Brianna) in a big way. We were all quite impressed after watching him perform in productions of *Pinocchio, The Sound of Music,* and *Peter Pan.*

Here's one thing I learned as a parent and a child of the universe: You can never get anyone to do anything by force. Years of trying with zero success is proof of this.

The "keys to the kingdom" lie in knowing that there is a vast difference between force and power. Force combines resistance with allowance (imagine two fists pushing against each other). Power—real power—combines allowance with intention. Allowance and inten-

You can never get anyone to do anything by force.

tion are energies that combine to produce a positive effect 100% of the time. This power is not demonstrated with physical prowess; instead, it comes from within, and everybody on the planet has it. The problem is that most people do not believe this, so it goes relatively unused for most of our lives.

Take back your power. Envision the situation as working out in your favor. Visualize exactly what you want to see happen until you are so clear about it that you can smell it, hear it, feel it, and touch it. Say what you want to see happen out loud, or silently, just before you go to bed, every day for five minutes. It is not a lot of time to sacrifice, considering what you will receive in return. Then relax and allow the miracle to unfold, as it will, in divine time—which, after all, is the only time there is.

MY WIFE'S AMAZING HEART

It Takes Effort

Spirit sometimes allows catastrophic things to happen to nudge us out of our comfort zone and really start to live. Sometimes the pain we feel helps us to place our trust in spirit instead of our attention on more money, more drugs, bigger houses, more sports, more movies, and more parties. For people like Jennifer and me, that comfort zone is not as "comfy" as all that. We have our struggles, but dealing with Jason's medical bills while losing income really propelled us to think on a more spiritual level.

I was rather excited when Jennifer found a job in an accounting firm, which appeared to have the hours she wanted and decent pay. It also had the added bonus of not being too far from home. She was not passionate about the actual work however (not being an accountant), and this lack of enthusiasm eventually became obvious at the office. It just wasn't going as smoothly as Jennifer had hoped it would.

I went to a spiritual advisor about something else a short time after my wife started with the accounting firm. When I mentioned how happy I was about my wife finding a job, the psychic said nothing but just looked at me sadly.

A few months later, my wife was fired for no particular reason. (At least they could not mistreat her anymore.) Even though I wanted to panic about the lack of money, I was resolved to be more trusting in life's process and relax more about facing such chancy situations. I "took my hand off the wheel" and turned it over to the "manager." I told

When we're ready to let go and let it happen, magic will occur.

Jennifer that it was a blessing in disguise, and even congratulated her. That may have surprised her, but everything worked out in the end.

Jennifer pulled out of her "underemployed" depression, as the painful process forced her to seek a somewhat more faith-based life—although she has always been a tough-minded realist, and probably always will be. She started to be more open to things like positive affirmations, healing music, and self-help books, eventually starting a little business that was run out of a day spa. It was a slow process. Jennifer wants to know that she is not being fooled by fly-by-night hipsters, and I don't blame her.

Then she experienced a real, live miracle. As they say in commercials (and in that song by Tammi Terrell and Marvin Gaye), "Ain't nothing like the real thing."

My beautiful wife was driving Brianna to a violin lesson. It was a particularly rainy night, and Jennifer was having a little trouble seeing the road. As she approached her exit, she misjudged the distance to the guard rail and rode the vehicle up and over the metal barrier, completely flipping the car. It landed upside down and was crushed beyond repair. A metal rod pierced through the roof and thrust downward, directly above where Brianna was strapped in place. The rod missed Brianna's skull by an inch or two at best. That was a miracle she will (obviously) never forget! They both walked away from the accident without a scratch—with the exception of a small cut on my wife's pinkie finger.

The hand of God had spared both my wife and our daughter. It was getting biblical. These types of life-changing events do happen. They force us to look at life differently and decide if everything we experience is random or if there is some hidden blueprint or plan. We have to ask if our intentions and expectations might be drawing certain events into our lives and driving other events away. It makes us wonder what this thing called the "Self" really is and if it can influence events at a distance or well into the future.

"Jennifer, you and Brianna not only lived through what should have been a fatal crash but walked away without a scratch. If that's not proof of a divine entity permeating everything in the universe, what is?" I went on to say that, "This should strengthen your faith that things happen when they are supposed to happen. Although it is challenging right now, there is always darkness before the dawn. Your perfect job will manifest when you simply ask for (and truly expect) the perfect job. Period! With true faith, you know that it will come at the perfect time and when it will benefit you the most."

We all tend to question the "when" and the "how." Unfortunately, this kind of doubt ultimately screws up our sense of self-worth and our hopes of accomplishing great things. When we're ready to let go and let it happen, magic will occur.

I held Jennifer's hands and said, "Please believe that the perfect opportunity for *you* is waiting for you to call it forth. Trust that God will bring it to you at the exact time it is supposed to come. I believe in you with every fiber of my being, and I believe in us. I believe we are truly blessed, and that the best is yet to come."

By the way, Jennifer finally got a new job, with good pay, 27 hours a week. They even let her choose the days she would work. It made it easier for her to do the things she loved with the family like playing "the mom" and "the chauffeur." It worked out according to what spirit wanted, according to a plan better than anything she could have written down on paper.

The Secret to a Good Marriage

My wife believes in positive thinking and creating the life you were meant to live, but she is careful not to go to extremes. One evening, after a real-estate seminar, I was tired, but Jennifer and I decided to watch *The Secret* on DVD. This was a replacement DVD because the first one didn't work. I knew I had to get up at 5 a.m., but I thought this would be inspirational for us. The DVD stalled for about

121

The universe will give you what you need but not always what you want.

10 minutes, and then the little rascal started working. Then it stopped, and then it started working but in the wrong place. Rewind stopped working, then fast forward jumped too far. We tried the laptop; no luck. Then the basement DVD player; it started working perfectly. Fifteen minutes into the movie, the power went off throughout the house due to a storm that had brewed.

Jennifer looked at me and said, "We know this stuff already. Let's go to bed!"

The universe will give you what you need but not always what you want. I *wanted* to see *The Secret*, but I *needed* to get some sleep. Yeah, yeah. I should have known better. So much for "forcing" the issue.

A Love Poem

Here is a poem I wrote for Jennifer. Perhaps it will give you a better sense of her than the stories I am telling. God knows the poem still cannot do her justice (but hey I'm trying here)!

How do I love thee?
Let me count the ways.
I love thee for being
The loving, supportive mother
That you are to our two beautiful children.
I love thee for putting up with my "trying to find myself" stage.
I love thee for the tireless ways
In which you schlep, cook, fold, make a living,
And still find time to help those who need it.
I love thee for being a caring and loving niece,
Daughter, daughter-in-law, friend, and wife.
I love thee for choosing ME to be the one

122

To spend the rest of your life with.
Your loving husband.

A year later, I wrote this:

I just want to tell you that I admire your courage.
I just want to tell you that I admire your kindness.
I want you to know that I'll always be here for you.
There is no one in this world that I have more faith in.
There is no one in this world that I would rather have as my soul
mate.

Miracles Come in All Sizes

I was about to leave work one day when Jennifer called. She told me that Ashley Tisdale, a celebrity whom my eight-year-old daughter was absolutely "nuts" about, was scheduled to appear at a local mall at 9:30 p.m. She would be signing autographs and shaking hands with fans like Brianna. Jennifer wanted to know if it would be all right if they went without me so I could babysit Jason.

I was caught a bit off guard by the short notice. It would break up my routine but, as usual, I asked spirit what would be the best solution for everyone involved. As so often happens, I received a spark of "daddy genius" in response. I guess someone up there loves children and wants to make them happy.

With a slight stutter, I answered, "Uh … sure, honey. On second thought, why don't you let me take her and you babysit Jason? It would make for some good daddy/daughter bonding!"

My wife agreed, and the plan was put into motion. Upon arriving home in record time, I washed up and proceeded to eat the already prepared meal waiting at the table. We quickly shoveled a few bites of spaghetti into our mouths and hurried to the car to begin our "adventure."

After all, as Brianna put it so poignantly, "This is the opportunity of a lifetime, Daddy!"

It was raining pretty hard, and it seemed as though the storm would only get worse before it got better. I made it to the mall in about 45 minutes, which was a qualifying track time, considering the weather. The fact that we were able to find a parking spot immediately and close to the entrance, when the parking lot was otherwise totally full, didn't faze my daughter in the least. It conformed to her expectations, as her mind was on one thing, and one thing only.

Everything appeared to be going as planned. We walked briskly into the mall and proceeded to look for prepubescents carrying signs that read, "We Love You, Ashley" and giggling with delight. My daughter spotted a few immediately, and we headed in that direction.

After about five minutes, we had seen quite a bit of the mall but no Ashley. I stopped a security guard and asked if he could direct me to where Ashley Tisdale was.

The answer was not to my daughter's liking: "Tisdale left about 15 minutes ago. She was signing autographs until about 7:00 but decided to head out early on account of the storm."

I looked at my watch. Sure enough, in what seemed like an almost mocking display of insubordination to Brianna's will, it read 7:18. My daughter was devastated. For a few minutes, she didn't say anything, and then the tears started flowing.

"Daddy! This really *was* the opportunity of a lifetime. What did I do wrong?"

How in the world does a parent explain to a kid—who, up until a few minutes earlier, was more elated than a homeless person locked in a walk-in pantry stocked with food—that life has a way of sometimes throwing you a curve ball? It can happen out of the blue, even when we are clearly expecting a fast ball straight down the middle.

I tried in vain to explain that things happen for a reason and that maybe something bad would have happened to either one of us if we got to see Ashley. I tried to explain that there are no coincidences, and that it's never about what happens to you in life but about your reaction to it that matters.

Yeah, right. Did you ever try explaining to your daughter that there will be another opportunity for a part in a different Broadway show in addition to the one she just lost? And after working her whole life for that audition? I grant you that it's not the same set of circumstances but, to a sweet eight-year-old girl, it might as well be. The ride home was not exactly what you might call a "bonding" moment, although in my heart I was kind of hoping that it would be.

Just as we arrived home, I remembered that, long ago, my aunt told me that she was roommates with Ashley Tisdale's grandmother in college. I made up my mind then and there that I was going to work a little "Daddy magic."

I went upstairs for some privacy and made a quick call to my aunt, giving her a synopsis of the whole tragedy.

"Let me call her," she said, "and I'll get back to you."

Within 10 minutes, I got a return call with some fairly encouraging news: We should wait about a week and "see what happens." My initial thought was that an e-mail would be nice, but a phone call would pretty much make a little girl's decade!

I had the urge to go through the mail for that day and noticed, on the top of the stack, some "junk" mail that simply asked, "Are you a seeker?" The contents basically underscored the fact that we can all be elevated by becoming aware of our spiritual essence, which essentially makes up our core, as opposed to our physical state of being. This essence is sometimes referred to as our soul, aura, connection to God, Christ consciousness, or any number of other references. The name we assign is not as important as the fact that we recognize such a thing, and then try to live life from the soul's perspective. At the very least, we can find a way to live in balance with the Ego's perspective.

Miracles come in all sizes, and some miracles are tailor made to our needs, meaning more to us personally than they would to anyone else. About 10 days later, Brianna received a mysterious package in the mail from someone whom she didn't know. When she opened it, she found a

Ironically, when we completely let go of the need to control every move we make, we will find that "miracles" are often commonplace.

glossy photo of Ashley Tisdale autographed personally to her. It wasn't exactly a sleepover with Tisdale herself but, to an eight-year-old girl, we're talking "over the top" epicness!

This story illustrates a point that miracles can and do happen on a daily basis, but they are often unrecognized as such because there are no 10 plagues, walking on water, or turning one loaf of bread into hundreds. There is, however, the power of our untapped spiritual energy—an energy that has been with humankind since the beginning of time. In fact, this power is who we truly are; in other words, *our essence.* A lot of it simply has to do with listening to the still, small voice within us.

The Old Testament and, in particular, the *Zohar* point to an example where Moses and the Israelites get to the Red Sea after crossing the desert.

The Egyptian army is in hot pursuit, and the people shout out to God, "Why are you doing this to us after coming all this way through the desert?"

The response from God that most of us are not taught in Sunday school is, "Why are you shouting at me? You were given the tools to get yourselves out of this situation, and all you need to do is use them!"

As the story goes (according to the *Zohar*), one man steps forth and enters the sea up to his knees, then his waist, his neck, and finally to the top of his head. At that precise moment, every ounce of doubt that a miracle would occur was vanquished. The sea parted, and the Israelites crossed. Can this be explained through a miracle or a manifestation through absolute faith in the divine that dwells within each and every one of us? Is there even a difference? Ironically, when we completely let go of the need to control every move we make, we will find that "miracles" are often commonplace.

HERE WE ARE AGAIN (THE BIG PICTURE)

Belief Is Everything

In the past few years, many moments of intense spiritual connection started happening more regularly as I became "consciously aware" of my higher Self. Everyone has—or, to put it another way, is made up of—a mind and a body. What we tend to "forget" about, or maybe even choose to deny, is the higher Self. The problem is that, when we finally *do* acknowledge it, we do so in many instances under periods of loss or danger.

There are many such ways we can say "hello" to this integral part of ourselves when not faced with these circumstances, such as during meditation or yoga, while listening to music, or even when taking a walk in the woods. Other ways might be while reading a good book, cooking a meal, or snuggling with a pet. My point is that we all "connect" in some way, and it's a matter of finding out how.

This Self (as opposed to self), however, is just as much a part of us as our Ego. In addition to the divine healing I received while listening to Andrea Bocelli, mentioned earlier, I also received a sort of "angel massage" while sitting alone and depressed in my car. I was waiting for Brianna to come out of her acting class. Like the previous time, I had a kind of spiritual orgasm, many times more powerful than the "typical" kind. Both times, I was alone in a car.

I believe that, during those times of asking for help from a higher source, I inadvertently raised the kundalini (primal energy located at

127

the base of the spine) through all of my chakra/energy centers until it burst right through the top center, known as the crown chakra. These moments leave me breathless and even tearful with joy, having made me humbly aware of the higher dimensions of reality that surround us all.

"Plugged In"

Sometimes I feel like I'm suddenly "plugged in" to a different reality—one that is full of playful possibilities—and I don't have to wait for scientific explanations. I just roll with it. It's a kind of awakening, of waking *up to* a dream where my inner thoughts and outer reality become creatively connected.

One time, I took my dad out for a birthday dinner while visiting in New Jersey. The restaurant was packed, and I didn't have a reservation. I told him not to worry, and that they would have a table for us. Sure enough, we walked in and got a table for two!

Some would laugh it off as coincidence, but I try to notice these things as signs that God is listening and perhaps even paving the way. Besides, as I already mentioned, I don't believe in coincidence, only in synchronicity.

Moving Mountains with the Mind

Meditating more and more often has allowed me to achieve a sort of "alpha" state, sometimes within seconds of starting the meditation. In the meditative state, the body syncs with the higher Self and experiences a kind of humming from the head to the toes. It's almost like being enveloped by millions of mosquitoes and not being bitten by any of them.

Stopping the rain on a number of occasions by "declaring it"—even casually throwing out the time it would occur—was something that always got a few blank stares. It seemed laughable at the time, and too much of a *coincidence* (sorry, but I have to use that word here) to give it a second thought; on the other hand, how can one explain the fact that it keeps happening? In this same state, I have also experienced a number of healings as well as an increase in psychic ability, which is hard to put into words. It's more like a "feeling" about the way things *really* are concerning this divine matrix of pure energy.

When I'm experiencing something in my reality, I tend to look at that reality as something I was meant to experience. It happened for a reason, for my benefit. It's *my* movie. The only person I should be concerned about is myself—not in the "selfish" way that most people think, but in a way that basically says, "If we are all connected through this divine matrix, then whatever happens to the collective happens at some level to me, and vice versa. I *am* truly my brother's keeper."

If you are doing something to me, I have the choice of seeing it as a lesson that I need to learn or seeing it as something else. I can react to it or not.

Most people will react like this: "If you are going to be aggressive towards me, I'm going to react with aggression."

A great rabbi once said, "Turn the other cheek."

However, it's difficult for many of us to put ourselves into this kind of mindset. Yes, it is possible, but I would be willing to wager that more people than not don't want to think about it. They don't realize that, if they are experiencing anything, it's because, at some point in time (through the Law of Attraction), they exuded that emotion/feeling/vibration and are *now* experiencing what they (either consciously or unconsciously) "put out."

I am not claiming to be different or more special in any way, shape, or form than anyone else on the planet. There are many instances where I *still* forget that I have the *option* of reacting with the Ego or with the Self. The point is, in fact, that everyone can tap into this kind of mindset just by asking, praying, and meditating with real conviction. I experienced many of these so-called miracles because I was open minded enough to believe that some experiences do not happen within the realm of the five senses but are perceived with another part of ourselves, which lies just beyond them. Let's call it "intuition," "a sixth sense," "spirit," or whatever. The label, once again, is not important.

Some experiences can't be explained in scientific terms. Try asking a skilled neurosurgeon to pinpoint a thought—not the center where the thought originated, which is difficult enough, or the firing of the neuron, but the *actual* thought. Get the picture?

In her book, *Dying to Be Me,* Anita Moorjani presents the analogy of walking around our whole lives in a dark warehouse filled with all kinds of treasures. The problem is that, with nothing to guide us but a tiny flashlight, we have no idea that these treasures surround us. Most of us don't even believe that they exist at all. When we transform from physicality (I prefer to use this word instead of death), we finally find the light switch. We don't need death to find that elusive switch because higher consciousness is present in every moment of our lives. We simply need to be aware of it.

The universe began as a dot, which contained all the matter that ever existed or ever will exist. A great singularity. The only difference between this dot and what exists now is that the space within the atoms was removed. What came forth from this cosmic "fireworks display" included the space. In fact, matter (ultimately existing as atoms) is so vacuous that it practically doesn't exist at all. Only energy exists, yet everything that comprises the universe is perceived by our brain as tangible, physical "stuff"—including, of course, *us.*

When talking about humans, the dilemma is that most conversations about our lives sooner or later will include what happens when our bodies begin to "permanently" break down. The problem in talking about death, however, is that, in order to define it, you must first define "you."

What are you? A mixture of energies following some vague blueprint no one completely understands? What really comprises the totality of who you think you are? If we replace everything in you except your brain, are you still you? Are you the same person you were yesterday? Who is the new you? Where do you begin, and where does your environment end? Depending on how we answer these questions, we

The only state that is "real" and unchanging is the soul/spirit/core essence.

may come to the startling conclusion that there is no death *per se* but only a transformation of energy from one state of being to another.

We can start with this premise: "Energy cannot be created or destroyed, it can only be changed from one form to another." You either believe this statement or not. It was spoken by Albert Einstein, supposedly one of the most intelligent humans who ever lived.

What do we mean by "change form"? Science has proven, and most of us believe, that the smallest unit of matter is the atom, and that the atom itself is comprised of subatomic particles, which are in turn made up of varying degrees of vibrations/frequencies. Depending on the intensity of the vibration, what we perceive is categorized as solid, liquid, or gas. These subatomic particles/waves, however, do not exist as physical entities. They follow a different set of laws than matter (a field known as "quantum physics/quantum mechanics"), and, when photographed, will leave only residual "trails" of their supposed images.

In addition, when observing an atom, we find that the relative distance between the orbit of electrons around its nucleus and the actual nucleus is somewhat equivalent to the distance between Pluto and the sun. If so, what does this space consist of? If nonphysical stuff called "energy" makes up all physical stuff (e.g., atoms), then we and everything in the universe are comprised of energy. So what is death? Can energy die? Or does it, as Einstein put it, "change form"?

The undying "you" that I am referring to is not a singularity; it is an energy field in context with other energy fields. You are a transient being comprised of body, mind, and soul. The only state that is "real" and unchanging is the soul/spirit/core essence; the name is irrelevant and only acts to negate (as Deepak Chopra would say). This essence is eternal. Everything else is constantly changing and in a state of flux. I am not the same person I was yesterday or will be next year. I am not pretending to be anything. I simply and exquisitely *am*.

The Political Power of the Enlightened Self

You cannot extinguish the flames of bigotry, hatred, jealousy, and intolerance by throwing more fuel into the inferno. Country after country continue to build their military might by increasing their war machines. They believe that "might makes right" and, with enough force, the enemy will succumb. What they cannot see is that no amount of money or armies can change the collective consciousness. It *must* change if the human race is to survive, and it *will* change if enough of us envision and *believe* it to be so.

The question is, "How?"

The answer is so simple and obvious that it seems trivial: "It all starts with the Self."

Humankind was made in the image and likeness of God. What can be said of this statement, and what comes to mind when you read these words? I would hazard to guess that when most of us read these words, images are conjured up of God as an old man with a white beard, ruling the universe from his ethereal plane.

A question was posed at my synagogue some time ago: "What does it mean when you hear the words, 'Humans were created in the image and likeness of God?'"

I raised my hand and offered the following (I'm paraphrasing a bit here): "We were created by (or came out of) an essence that endowed us with the same qualities to create as it possesses. We are therefore cocreators with the Creator, and, as such, are creating our realities in every moment in the eternal moment of now. If enough of us realize that the collective consciousness can and *must* change in order for the human race to survive, we will reach critical mass, and evolve to the next level." Needless to say, I got a few blank stares out of that one!

In fact, everything in existence started as a thought (including the universe itself), which, upon observation and according to quantum theory, manifested itself into physicality.

The Creator within All of Creation

There is much evidence to suggest that everything we see (i.e., that exists as solid, liquid, or gas) is made up of the same atomic material but exists in different densities throughout the universe. This material is nothing more than energy vibrating at specific frequencies relative to the number and arrangement of the elements that make up the material.

One premise, believed by billions of people around the world, is that a higher power is responsible for creating all that is. A skeptic may say that "all that is" started from what has become known as the Big Bang Theory.

Who is to say, however, that when in Genesis, God said, "Let there be light," the light and subsequent explosion we call the Big Bang were not initiated by God himself? If not initiated through this divine intelligence, than *what did* initiate the beginning of everything, including space and time?

That being said, it can thereby be proposed that this universal intelligence known as "God" by the vast majority of the world is in fact the Creator. He created us in his likeness, not meaning that we look like God but that we "cocreate" as God creates. By simply observing what exists in the world today, we can declare this to be so. In fact, everything in existence started as a thought (including the universe itself), which, upon observation and according to quantum theory, manifested itself into physicality.

To put it another way, everything that exists was once merely an unmanifested idea or a notion. Furthermore, if we believe that God is indivisible, than God must also exist within all things physical and nonphysical. For God to exist outside of us would imply divisibility and

Good and bad are quite simply our value judgments about a particular event or circumstance, relative to how others view that circumstance.

negate this definition. Oneness by its very nature cannot be twoness. Taken to the nth degree, and thought to be the case in Buddhism, even substance and consciousness are inextricably linked and cannot be separated.

If one believes that God can manifest everything and anything that exists, and is everywhere at the same time, this higher power is, by default (as I mention above), within every one of us. We are, in fact, part of the divine—not just figuratively. This being the case, we can and will manifest whatever it is we seek to bring into reality. You may not always get what you *think* you want, but you will always get what you *create*; in other words, what you call forth with your thoughts combined with your feelings/emotions.

Catholics believe in the Father, the Son, and the Holy Ghost; psychiatrists believe in the id, the ego, and the superego; poets believe in the mind, the heart, and the soul. Why is it so hard to fathom that God can be explained in this way? That her body is everything made manifest, and his mind and spirit are everything else—the "all" that is, was, and ever will be?

I went to see a talk by Wayne Dyer before he died, and even got to chat with him for a few minutes. He was a very down-to-earth guy. I'll never forget what he said to the audience that day about who and what we really are, as opposed to what we "perceive" ourselves to be.

"When you are thinking about all this God stuff, and the divine matrix, you may get your thoughts mixed up with the terminology. So, let me make it a little easier for you. Think about the ocean. You have a glass, and you take that glass and dip it into the ocean. What do you have in that glass? Do you have something like the ocean? Similar to the ocean? No, you have *the ocean*. It's not as big as the ocean, not as powerful, but it is the ocean, made up of everything the ocean is made of.

"Each one of us may use a different size glass. The shape and color of the glass may even vary, but these points are irrelevant once the glass of ocean water is poured back into its source. Once it is [when you are 'in death'], are you able to extract that exact same glass of water back out? No! It becomes one with the *entire* ocean—as big and as powerful. What I am proposing is that *you* are that glass of water. You are existing as that glass of water *right now*."

Good and bad are quite simply our value judgments about a particular event or circumstance, relative to how others view that circumstance. The event itself, as discussed earlier, is always neutral. Similarly, how we react emotionally to everything that is happening around us is controlled by our Egoic mind. When we disassociate from the Egoic mind, all that is left is consciousness. We can then perceive ourselves to be the consciousness, witnessing how we react to the event. This is the beginning of awareness.

In his book, *A New Earth*, Eckhart Tolle sums up all of this quite nicely. He alludes to the fact that more and more people are discovering how to do this, creating "pockets" of consciousness around the globe. The hope is that the human race will choose to continue this evolutionary process—unless, of course, we don't!

The conscious mind (not brain) in its true form is not really a cognitive thinking machine—as most of us perceive it to be—but an essence that makes up who we really are *at our core*. To quote Neale Donald Walsch, it is "the thought behind the thought." Not the content, but the *context* of what makes up consciousness itself. In other words, the "I am" observer witnessing that which is *doing* the witnessing! For an in-depth explanation, one can refer to *The Discovery: Revealing the Presence of God in Your Life* by Dr. David R. Hawkins.

> Are we too far gone? Yes and no. If we don't hit critical mass in a spiritual direction, we *will* hit critical mass in another direction.

When someone asks what you do for a living, you quickly respond that you are an accountant or an engineer, and then you end up playing the role that an accountant or an engineer is supposed to play. Most of the time, we even believe that this is truly who we are and, eventually, the rest of the world comes to believe it as well. This is *not* who you are; it is simply part of *what you do*. With all due respect to accountants (myself being one) and engineers, we are not human doings. We are human *beings*!

In our society, we go one step further and equate degrees, titles, permits, and licenses with the power to *do things* and therefore *to be*. These strings of letters easily attach to us. Instead of saying, "This is my fellow being, also created in God's image" or even, "This is my friend Scott," they become "RN," "MD," "MSW," or "PhD."

One night, I called my sister Lisa and told her that I was proud of her for who she was, not what she did, or the fact that she did or did not have six or seven letters after her name.

She responded with, "No one has ever told me that before."

I suddenly felt a closeness to her that had not been there before. I hung up, feeling pretty good about myself. She is on her way. We've all been through so much together. Our love for each other has been the glue that prevented our worlds from falling apart at the seams.

State of the World

I think we're are on the cusp of going in one direction or another. We are on the precipice. The terrorism, the bigotry, and the poverty are here to shake out the garbage under the rug.

Is it possible? Sure. I think we can go in either direction. When we talk about an era of peace and love, I think of that as stemming from a messianic age. Whether a single messiah can bring that into being remains to be seen.

I do believe, however, that we are moving towards critical mass. Maybe terrorism, bigotry, and pride (of the Ego) are simply speeding up the process of evolution. Could it be that it's necessary to experience all of this in order to finally make that quantum leap into the "higher consciousness" levels that Jesus, Moses, Buddha, Lao Tzu, and others spoke of? It comes to a point where we've gone beyond the conditioning and have tapped into that divine essence we are all a part of.

Are we too far gone? Yes and no. If we don't hit critical mass in a spiritual direction, we *will* hit critical mass in another direction. We are all going back to the source. Either we experience total destruction and annihilation, and then start over like the biblical flood or Atlantis, or it won't have to get to that point. If enough people can wake up, realize their connection to the whole, and reach a different critical mass, we will take it to another level. We will turn it around. I know that it is possible to go in the direction of "raising the collective consciousness."

The question remains, "Will we be able to (literally) save ourselves before we get to where we appear to be going?"

In metaphysics, there is the world of the absolute and the world of the relative—of duality. The mind, body, spirit triune, which comprises who we actually are, exists in both worlds simultaneously. In the dimension of the absolute, there is no "time," and everything has already happened—the apocalypse as well as saving the world through our own divine love and understanding, another genesis of sorts. It's all in the eternal moment of *now*. (Thank you, Eckhart Tolle and Neale Donald Walsch once again!)

We are becoming more aware of what lies beyond the illusion. One person isn't going to make this happen. A movement will make it happen—a revolution—that is waking people up and showing them that they can do this. We can actually move beyond our trifles. I truly believe it can and will happen because more and more of us are starting to wake up to the possibilities: Deepak Chopra, Carolyn Myss, the late Wayne Dyer, Gregg Braden, Rhonda Byrne (see "Helpful Resources" on page 159). These names are fast becoming more commonplace. People no longer discount their words or dismiss them as "out there" or New Age. We really can't afford to do this.

Would you rather sit back and say, "This is it. There is nothing more to do," and let the hatred and poverty take over? We *do* have enough time. We *do* have enough money. We *do* have enough love to really change things. We *do* have enough of everything.

The question is, "Do we really want to change things?" Are we so wrapped up and "comfortable" with ourselves, so busy with our lives, that we don't want to "make waves"? We may be happy with the way things are because change (for many of us) takes effort and can sometimes be scary and even daunting.

People say, "It's unfortunate that there is terrorism, but I have to keep my job. I have to pay my mortgage." They don't want to rock the boat.

This wave has been building for some time, but it is now starting to gain more and more power (incrementally); pretty soon, it will break, and it will roll. To be honest, that may not be a bad thing. Everything that's going on around us (today) is simply the dirt being "beaten" out of the carpet, *not* the coming of the Four Horsemen of the Apocalypse. People all over the world panicked just before Y2K (the year 2000), with stories of computers crashing on a worldwide scale. This lead to a water crisis, food shortages, and another "energy crisis"—you name it. The media fueled the hype, and we bought into it hook, line, and sinker.

We are all searching for something deeper. It begs the question, "Is this all there is?"

The Kabbalah has really opened up some doors for me in this regard with insights that I have shared in this book. In particular, I want to say that we *can* merge spirituality and entrepreneurship. The most important thing I've discovered, however, is that, if you want to grow, you have to *change*. This, my friends, has been one of the most difficult things for me to accept, and I'm still working on it.

138

We are all searching for something deeper. It begs the question, "Is this all there is?"

We all need to subdue this thing called the E-G-O before it "takes over." In order to do this, we need to move outside of our comfort zone. Up to this point, it has been the most difficult thing for me to do, but I have resolved that, in order to move forward—to really grow—I must find a way.

TURNING DREAMS INTO REALITIES

From Whence I Came

I am God's man, who could dare to defy me ... the
sun of hopes is out in all directions ... my intentions
are solid, and there is courage in every step ... I have
set forth today to write my own destiny.

—From *Dhoom 3*

The above quote was a tattoo on a young man's arm, which I noticed while waiting in line at the dry cleaners. I admired it, and then boldly went up to the guy and asked him about it. He was only too happy to satisfy my curiosity. On the way home from the dry cleaners, I was inspired to write down my thoughts. The poem merges some of my thoughts with a quote from William Shakespeare:

You can only learn from the past.
You can only live in the present.
The future, however, is for us to create.

Celebrate your life and every experience you've ever had.
Celebrate every experience you ever will have.
Be grateful for everything, even your garbage,

*For the contrast will allow you to see what it is that you truly
desire.*

Accolades and success fuel the Ego.
Passion for knowledge fuels the soul.
Merge these two for the sake of the Self, and you awaken the Self.
Merge these for the sake of another, and you awaken both of you.

I shall not follow the Joneses, or even keep up with them.
I shall be the Joneses.
Above all ... do not be afraid to humbly speak your truth.

> *They say some men are born great,*
> *some achieve greatness, and some have*
> *greatness thrust upon them.*
>
> —William Shakespeare

I say follow your path, and greatness shall be yours, on your terms,
and in your own way.

Yesterday has faded into memory. Tomorrow is a new day and
another opportunity to create.

Our life experiences aren't just processed with our minds; our
minds *create* our life experiences. To put this another way, we create
our reality through nothing more than our thoughts. You can choose
to be the *cause* of what becomes your life, or you can choose to be the
effect of it. Either way, you always have a choice.

God does not reward or punish. She does not choose sides but
instead has given humanity the ability to choose. Everything in life—
every action we take, every decision we make—comes down to one
of two choices: We can either choose in a proactive state of being or
choose in a reactive state. When we choose the proactive approach,
we are emulating the energy that brought us and everything else forth
from a singularity, one million times smaller than a pinhead, into the
known universe. When we choose from a reactive state, we call forth

the chaos that will eventually ensue. Chaos is its own punishment. Choosing to be proactive, and in total alignment with the all of everything (the I AM presence) is its own reward.

Start each day by "prepaving" your experiences. You can do this by thanking the universe in advance for getting through your day with grace and ease, and by visualizing through the day ahead that everything is being worked out smoothly. It is not fatalistic; it is totally creative.

I have a friend who kept running into "knuckleheads" at Giant foods. Nearly every time he went into that store, some overzealous person would practically fight him for the last of the 50-cent avocados!

I said that, if he had meditated each morning and prepaved the shopping trip, the altercations would more than likely not have happened, and those people would not have even been at the Giant that day. I urged him to try it—not by worrying that those people would not be at the store that day (as it might act as a negative visualization and actually attract them) but by concentrating on what he *did* want, which was to run into nice, helpful people. I'm sure you can guess what happened the next time he went to the store!

Focus on what you *do* want instead of what you *don't*. In doing so, you generally find that you attract that which you think about. On the other hand, thinking about the "lack" of what you want is quite tempting and will ... well, you get the idea.

I reminded my buddy of our "night out" earlier that year. I had prepaved this important trip to a restaurant that we both liked using visualization, which managed to get us into that busy place without a reservation. I didn't react with disappointment and worry when we drove up to a full parking lot because, when I do that, I take myself out of alignment with divine energy. I simply looked at the hostess with calmness and confidence, all the while envisioning a positive outcome.

"We need a table for two."

I have been told that the higher the vibration you live in, the greater the impact your thoughts have on the reality you're creating for yourself.

Without missing a beat, we were led to the only open table in the house. It just "happened" to be a table for two!

I truly feel that I am approaching the tipping point. However, if I so much as *think* one tiny thought that is out of alignment with the oneness, I am blasted for it. In the past, when I was ignorant about the way things really worked, I could worry all day and never experience the mental pounding that I seemed to be taking on at that time. The more light I let in, the more I am tested. Yet I am grateful for the opportunity to have my garbage pointed out so I can transcend it.

Here's one thing that I am curious about: My upper teeth have almost a constant dull pain, a kind of throbbing. I wear a mouth guard at night, but this seems to occur during the day. Is it being caused by me, or is it energy from outside myself that I am somehow attracting?

I have been told that the higher the vibration you live in, the greater the impact your thoughts have on the reality you're creating for yourself. In that case, when we aren't in alignment, it is immediately obvious. The greater the power, the greater the responsibility.

Why the teeth? Jaw stress. Sometimes the energy pushes up quite strongly from within. The thing to do is to meditate and move your head and neck around to let it loose.

Choose faith over fear.

Choose certainty instead of doubt.

Choose to see beauty, even in the most morose of circumstances.

Choose optimism when the world appears chaotic.

Choose charity over selfish purposes.

Choose peace of mind amidst anything that would give cause to negate it.

Choose to be proactive instead of reactive.

Choose to let go of that which no longer serves you.

Choose to know with conviction that, through divine grace, you were, are, and always will be the master of your domain.

Opinions are like underwear: Everyone seems to have one, and they're constantly changing. In any event one would be wise to:

Watch your thoughts, they become your words.
Watch your words, they become your actions.
Watch your actions, they become your habits.
Watch your habits, they become your character.
Watch your character, it becomes your destiny.

—Frank Outlaw

At the risk of sounding redundant, it's never about what happens to you or what other people are doing or not doing. It's about how you react to it that really matters. You always have a choice as to how you are going to respond to any circumstance or event.

Creating Reality

When it comes to our life circumstances, why don't we always get what we intend to "create"? Is it that we are sending out a vibration, either consciously or subconsciously, that is opposite of our intention?

We know that a particular frequency will inevitably attract a "like" vibration. Is the "vibe" we are sending out a higher frequency or lower than the image we are constructing in our minds? Seen from this perspective, we can understand why a great master said, "Do unto others as you would have them do unto you." It was good advice in order to be moral or just and would later be known as the Law of Attraction. This law operates the same way it has since the dawn of time: You get *back* what you send *forth!*

Here's the bottom line: We were given the ability to create our reality, starting with our thoughts about that reality, whether or not we know this to be true. This ability to choose how we will "perceive"

I am aware that those of you who refuse to live outside of your perspective paradigms *at any cost* will not be entirely convinced of physicality seen from this particular point of view.

something—anything, really—will never be interfered with, under any circumstances, by the source that granted it.

The question now arises, "Why do the circumstances even exist that would warrant responses to 'negative' life events such as anger, contempt, judgment, and sadness?"

The answer becomes quite obvious when we look deeper, yet it continues to elude us. God neither allows nor condemns; God merely observes. Humankind will create at one level through the collective consciousness and at another level through the individual mind. It's as complex and as simple as that. We can create our world using fear (the lower frequencies of hatred, judgment, and so forth) or by using love (the higher frequencies of kindness, respect, and tolerance for others unlike ourselves). Regardless of our actions, the qualities of these frequencies will determine the quality of the outcome.

I am aware that those of you who refuse to live outside of your perspective paradigms *at any cost* will not be entirely convinced of physicality seen from this particular point of view. My job, however, is not to convince you that what I believe is true. It is more about looking at the same things we have always looked at from a different perspective.

In order to do this, we need to "change the lens" through which we view that perspective. When this occurs, we will clearly see that *separation from each other and everything else that makes up the universe is an illusion, and that this is not just a figurative reality but a physical one.*

This very issue is what has divided humanity (both metaphorically as well as physically) for millennia. I have attempted to explain this from a somewhat "nontraditional" point of view, I grant you. However, with all due respect to each and every spiritual tradition out there, doing what *actually* works should be given as much consideration as doing *what we are told* works. By being active participants in the "process" each and every day (i.e., living with and "on" purpose) as well as paying a bit more attention to the agenda of the Self, and maybe a bit less to the agenda of the Ego, we can engage ourselves fully in this experience we call life.

Here's an analogy: If you are having trouble seeing in the dark, instead of blaming someone or something else, or cursing the darkness, try removing your glasses and replacing them with infrared military goggles. These goggles are not magic; they are simply a technology, enabling you to see things that were actually there all along.

The Whole Is Greater than the Sum of Its Parts

Many of us would say that we believe with certainty in the statement, "God is infinite and has no boundaries." Yet more than a few might retract a bit if we pointed out that, if this is so, then God is also in us. In fact, the words "infinite and has no boundaries" should and do mean "in" and "throughout" every living and nonliving thing in the universe. Would it be a stretch to even say "makes up" the universe? This would then include our thoughts and everything in the nonphysical and metaphysical dimensions as well.

If you believe that everything is ultimately energy (a point that can in fact be proven through quantum physics), then there *cannot be* any separation between us and anything else in the physical, nonphysical, and metaphysical dimensions. This will hopefully shed a bit more light on the biblical verse, Mark 12:30-31: "You shall love your neighbor as yourself." This sentence *literally* implies that you and your neighbor are one and the same! When we see ourselves as standing waves of energy, this is a reasonable idea—not just a nice metaphor or a play on words.

This kind of paradigm may be hard for many of us to swallow, so let me try to elaborate by using those analogies I spoke of. Think of a massive jigsaw puzzle with an almost infinite number of pieces (let's say 10 x 10 to the billionth power). Each piece interlocks with every other

If one piece out of the trillions of pieces is missing, the puzzle is not complete; it cannot be whole.

piece to form this massive, beautiful mosaic. Each piece is individual unto itself, uniquely shaped, with distinct colors and patterns, yet relies on every other interlocking piece to give it meaning relative to the whole puzzle. If one piece out of the trillions of pieces is missing, the puzzle is not complete; it cannot be whole. This would make every piece of the puzzle important in its own right, no matter the shape, size, or color.

A second example might be if one pictures an apple pie. The pie can be cut into many pieces, Yet, left in the container, it appears to be whole. It is only until you remove a piece that the pie becomes "unwholey" (pardon the pun). The individual piece of apple pie may be a slightly different size and shape than the piece sitting next to it, but it is made up of the exact same thing!

I hope that you can see where I'm going with all of this, as I need you to read between the lines. As I stated earlier, if you believe Einstein's theory of conservation of mass and energy, then you can see by default that, if we are ultimately *made* of energy (to include our thoughts), it would be possible to simply transform our energy from physical to nonphysical frequencies. When we perceive ourselves as making this "transformation," we are poured back into the source from whence we came—just like that glass of ocean water.

At that point, for all intents and purposes, we *are* the ocean, not just the glass of ocean water. It would be impossible to get that same glass of water back *out* of the ocean; in other words, there is no separation. There never was. The good part is that we don't have to experience death as we know it in order to understand this analogy, although many of us still believe that we do. In fact, the sheer number of recorded "near-death" experiences since 1992, and the remarkable similarities among these accounts by millions of individuals, are testament to this fact. I have no doubt that many more cases around the world will be documented as well from this point forward.

Orange Juice Discourse

A Zen master held a beautiful orange in his right hand and walked over to a monk, who was having trouble keeping his temper during the common times and at meals.

The master touched the monk's shoulder with his left hand and said, "Tenzin?"

"Yes, Roshi!"

"If I hold an orange in my hand and squeeze it, what comes out?"

"Orange juice, Roshi!"

"That is correct. Does it matter if it is squeezed when it's cold or hot outside, or who is squeezing it?"

"No, Roshi!"

"Sometimes you are like a beautiful orange, Tenzin."

"How is that, Roshi?"

"When you are squeezed, you expel whatever is inside you. If you are filled with anger, depression, anxiety, or rage, that is what will come out of you when circumstances tighten you in their vice-like grip. On the other hand, if you are filled with peace and love and tranquility, then no matter how hard people squeeze you, that is what will come forth. It does not matter what the other person says or does. What matters is how you react to it."

"Roshi, what is real?"

"That which never changes. All else is illusion, Tenzin. Always remember that."

Staring Down Death

My roommate from college and I took a canoe trip down the Brandywine River near Downingtown, Pennsylvania. We both stared death in the face as we got swamped in the strongest part of the river. The canoe took a beating, but we were both wearing life

It's pretty cool once you start to get into alignment with spirit.

vests. (I was hesitant about wearing the vest at first but was convinced that it was a "good" idea; otherwise, I'm sure the outcome would not have been so … good.) A boulder snapped a piece of beechwood on the hull like it was a toothpick. We lost an oar, which wasn't funny, and two straps, which held the canoe to the jeep. Freezing and covered with mud, we somehow carried the canoe back to the jeep.

We were having a good time, cruising down the river *just moments earlier,* enjoying the sight of herons, multicolored swallows, and hollowed-out trees. A lone guitar player sat on his porch, strumming his instrument (eerily similar to a scene out of *Deliverance*). We listened to the owner of the paddle-boat business as she pointed to a nearby dam. She explained how two kayakers "took their very last excursion" just a few weeks back when they went over it, after drinking a bit too much, and misjudged the swiftness and power of the current. "Locals" on the banks gave us bad directions and then, out of nowhere, all Hell broke loose! I had slept only two hours the night before, waking to the sound of wild birds chirping a sweet melody. Just a few hours later came the whitewater experience for contrast. It made me appreciate life all the more. Ah … the yin and yang.

The Dalai Lama

When asked what surprised him most about humanity, the 14th Dalai Lama answered, "Man. Because he sacrifices his health in order to make money. Then he sacrifices money in order to recuperate his health. Then he is so anxious about the future that he does not enjoy the present, the result being that he does not live in the present or the future; he lives as if he is never going to die, and then dies having never really lived."

I showed this to an office associate at the telecom company where I worked as an accountant, and she wanted to make a copy.

She then looked at me and said, "Hey, Mikey. We think *you're* the Dalai Lama of EHN Systems!"

I just folded my hands together, bowed, and thanked her. As soon as she left, I allowed myself an impish grin, and then went back to work.

Moving Out of Harm's Way

It's pretty cool once you start to get into alignment with spirit. You start releasing those nasty little phobias and hidden agendas. I recall how an office mate from many years ago was emitting a bit too much negative energy, and it was starting to affect my energy field even though I was trying hard not to let it in. This negative energy started to manifest into physical symptoms, such as acid reflux and breathing troubles. I know that I was put there, in that situation, to learn how to transcend this kind of behavior. Maybe I was there to teach others how to do the same thing. It worked! I realized that the universe acts in the same way as a mirror does: You get back what you put out.

Every day the barrage of anger, complaints, and resentment kept coming, and every day I tried my best to ignore them. I started to visualize my office mate's office being moved, or my office being moved, so that we would not be so close anymore. However, I didn't want to manifest a new job quite yet, especially not just to remove myself from this particular individual.

Two days later, I got word that my entire department would be moving to a new office down the road, right across from where my mom and aunt lived, so I could go there for lunch if I needed to. The office had just been remodeled and boasted a really nice gym. It was a win-win for everyone. The offices were much bigger, and the office-mate arrangement would change. Coincidence?

Anger

braham-Hicks seminars (see "Helpful Resources" on page 159) speak a lot about moving through the levels of vibration from the lowest to the higher frequencies. Anger is actually a step in the *right* direction if you're coming from despair. It's a step up from depression and one step below frustration. We can go from despair, right through depression, and straight to anger; after that, from anger to frustration, and then onto hope. I truly hope that all who experience suffering come to clarity. We often deserve way more than we allow ourselves.

What I Learned the Hard Way

ou will forever be presented with various life experiences. They are neither good nor bad, neither stressful nor calming. They are simply life experiences. How we perceive them is totally up to us.

We always have a choice about how we react to each and every situation the universe presents to us. Be thankful for every single thing in your life (including your challenges) for they allow you to grow and evolve.

Be present when you think about what is happening around you.

Don't waste your energy worrying about the past or concerning yourself with the future. Think about what you *do* want (with feeling) instead of the *lack* of it, and that will become your physical experience. Be persistent and keep the faith at all cost. Never give up!

Be heart-centered as opposed to head-centered.

Your Ego will throw you off course, but your heart never will.

Try to find time to meditate every day, even if only for 10 minutes.

Try reading occasionally instead of watching TV or finding out about what Dave Jones ate for dinner last week on Facebook.

Shut off the news, and stop letting negativity in.

Be present when you think about what is happening around you.

Stop talking about anything negative or about anyone in a negative light, except to clarify a point, and then move on. You will always receive back what you put out. There are no exceptions.

Observe, but try not to judge. Allow each person to walk their own path.

> *We acquire wisdom in three ways. Through reflection,*
> *it is the noblest. Through imitation, it is the easiest.*
> *Through experience, it is the bitterest.*
>
> —Confucius

Three Things You Need to Know

There are only three things you need to know. Everything else is filler.

1. You have an inner power that, when harnessed, allows you to transcend anything and attract whatever it is that you desire. Everyone else has this power too. The difference is that many people may not know that, and now you do.

2. You are loved in ways you can't even begin to imagine. If you can accept yourself, you'll find that others can accept you as well. If someone else can't, you should stop concentrating on trying to change their "movie" and concentrate on *yours*.

3. Your thoughts create your reality 100% of the time. Be consciously aware, therefore, to think about what you *do* want to attract (e.g., health, abundance, peace, and love) instead of what you don't. You are worthy, whether or not you know this to be true, *exactly* the way you are. Once you understand this and truly believe it, negative thinking becomes a thing of the

past. If you do not like what you have just created, simply know that you have somehow attracted it (as part of your learning experience as a worthy person). Once you take ownership of it, you can easily release it. Now you are free to create exactly what you *do* want.

You Have Everything You Need

You have everything you need inside of you to become whatever you wish to become. Stop thinking about spirituality as if it is some class at a community college, and try to start living its precepts. Every morning, just before you get out of bed, thank God for everything she blessed you with.

For the obstacles that beset you and the difficult people in your life, ask, "Why is this in my movie, and what do I have to learn from it?"

Then, thank God for all of the wonderful things you are about to receive in the future, and know with every fiber of your being that they are coming to you in perfectly divine time.

Finally, prepare your path for the day by thinking, "Serendipitous and synchronistic things will happen to me today to propel me forth in my quest for total fulfillment. Whoever comes into my life is there to help me, so that I in turn can help others."

As you move through this glorious experience of physicality, realize that pitfalls and setbacks are just another part of the experience. You cannot change what is, but you do not have to give it power. In some instances, these so-called "setbacks" can even act to give you much *more* resolve in order to achieve what you set out to do. If that means making cream cheese, then make that cream cheese with all of the passion you can muster. The amount of love you put into whatever you are doing will determine the end result.

Finally, don't just give lip service to the expression "carpe diem." Honor it. It should not be death that you fear the most; instead, it should be waking up one day and discovering that you haven't really lived at all. Know that these little "challenges," when overcome, will act to make the dream that much sweeter. Take that chance on life. It's calling you, and it's a bet that's in the bag. I dare you.

This Is the House that Mike Built

This is the death that gave rise to the birth
That led to the journey for all it's worth
That laid the foundation and helped to construct the house that Mike built.

This is the grandfather whose life became shattered
When his son was removed and nothing else mattered
That gave birth to the father who gave birth to the son
Who was riddled with guilt just about from day one
That also helped to add and give rise to the very house that Mike built.

This is the wife who married the father
Who went without sleep but didn't seem bothered
That is until asked how she felt about life
And said rather sadly, "I'm done with this strife."

It's time once again to return to the source
My soul has played through and run its due course
I've also helped you, my son, to build up this wonderful house
So hold onto your glass and drink a toast to your life.

With its smiles and giggles and its pain and its strife
Remember that always if we don't like our spin
Turn the bad into good, turn the lose into win.

This is the son who was born in the spring
Who showed us it's all about what we can bring
To the table of life that follows unending,

We can finally rest and let go of pretending.

So think deeply on this, and it all will make sense
We don't have to live under some false pretense
We each, all of us, have a house to create
From the bricks of our lives, not relying on fate
So stand strong and relinquish your worries and fears
It's not the years in your life but the life in your years!

EPILOGUE

They say a journey of 1,000 miles begins with a single step. That single step, however, will never be taken unless one makes a conscious decision to participate in the journey in the first place. My journey, along with everyone else's on the planet, began not with my physical birth but with a metaphysical decision to experience life at the physical level (thus giving over our temporary allegiance to the dimension of the physical). We choose our parents (paint, palette, and paper) but do not choose what picture we are going to paint, until we make the ultimate decision to live within the illusion of form.

Although this may seem a bit far-fetched to many people, and pure folly to others, I can assure you that many of us (today) are not in the least bit amused or surprised. With the likes of (the now late) Wayne Dyer, Gregg Braden, Eckhart Tolle, Deepak Chopra, and Neale Donald Walsch blazing the trail, metaphysics, spirituality, and self-actualization are no longer buzz words for woo-woo, fantasy, "keep away from that nut job" kind of stuff. We've come a long way from the hippie, love-child, tree-hugger days and have graduated to experiences beyond our five senses, some of us with PhDs in the metaphysical sciences.

All of us have a chance to create our own realities—not based on a limited set of circumstances but on the infinite power of our own thoughts. When combined with a conscious awareness of the feelings associated with such thoughts, we transform the Law of Attraction into the Law of Creation. At such a point, we make manifest (in physical form) that which was once just an idea or a notion. We are given the chance to fulfill our destiny in this lifetime, or the next, or quite possibly the one after that. It's entirely up to us.

Take some time to appreciate every moment of this wonderful gift we call "life," my friends. Above all, don't die with the music still playing in your head.

I stand alone in the shadow of this massive mountain undaunted, knowing with a calm certainty that … *I AM.*

Always and forever.

HELPFUL RESOURCES

For more inspirational quotes, images, and other resources designed to help in the process of self-actualization, visit heaveniswithin.net. This site was designed to raise the consciousness of the planet … one human at a time.

Here is a brief synopsis, listed alphabetically, to help you better understand the people whom I've referenced in this book:

ABRAHAM-HICKS: Abraham is reported to be a "collective" of consciousness from the nonphysical dimension, representing infinite intelligence. This collective was discovered by Jerry and Esther Hicks and is said to communicate through Esther. Esther, however, never actually uses the word "channeling" because she believes that using particular labels "muddies" the experience itself. There were, and continue to be at the time this book was published, Abraham-Hicks seminars (now with just Esther) throughout the United States.

GREGG BRADEN: Like many other spiritual leaders of our day, Braden did not start that way. He was a computer geologist back in the '70s and a senior liaison with the air force in the '80s. Braden is internationally recognized as one of the foremost leaders in bridging science with spirituality.

RHONDA BYRNE: Byrne is the creator and executive producer of the runaway hit movie, *The Secret,* as well as the author of the book by the same title. The film was released in 2006, using Vividas technology, and immediately went virile, captivating millions of viewers around the globe. Byrne was named in "The Time 100: The People Who Shape Our World." She appeared on *The Oprah Winfrey Show* with four teachers from the film *The Secret* and was on the *New York Times* bestseller list for 190 weeks.

PETE CARROLL: After a noteworthy but challenging start as an athlete, Carroll became one of the most successful football coaches of our time. The early years of 2000–2001 saw his University of Southern California Trojans team going 2-5; then, Carroll led the team to 67-7 out of the following 74 games. In 2010, he became the head coach for the Seattle Seahawks. Carroll is also known to be a humanitarian and a philanthropist. He started the program "A Better Seattle" to help reduce and prevent gang violence in the Seattle area.

WAYNE DYER: Inspirational speaker, author, and one of the most prominent self-help gurus to date, Dr. Dyer was known as the "master of motivation." It is estimated that his book, *Your Erroneous Zones*, has sold nearly 35 million copies. He was a college professor prior to his public-speaking career. Wayne passed on to bigger adventures in September 2015 at his home in Maui. He was diagnosed with leukemia some years earlier, but the official coroner's report indicated that he died of a heart attack in his sleep. It also indicated that there wasn't a trace of leukemia in his body.

NEVILLE GODDARD: Philosopher, metaphysical writer, and one of the founders of the 20th century's New Age movement, Goddard professed that visualization and mantras, for example, were not enough to manifest from thought. He believed that adding the *feeling* of what it was like to *already have* what you chose to manifest is required to create it, which is essentially the most important part of the equation.

LAIRD HAMILTON: As coinventor of "tow-in" surfing, Hamilton holds many records in the sport of surfing. He wrote the book, *Force of Nature: Mind, Body, Soul, And, of Course, Surfing,* and is known to be a "spiritual entrepreneur." Hamilton, like Eckhart Tolle, was also featured in Oprah Winfrey Network's production of *Oprah Presents Master Class in 2012.*

LIZ MURRAY: Despite being raised by drug-addicted parents, Murray is a Harvard University graduate who was homeless just previous to being accepted into the prestigious school. She is an inspirational speaker and the founder and director of Manifest Living, and has even had a made-for-TV film done about her life called *Homeless to Harvard.*

G. M. RAO: Born and raised in India, this billionaire tycoon started his career as a mechanical engineer. From there, he became involved with trading commodities and divested into acquiring businesses and other assets. Eventually, Rao started the GMR Group, which today operates India's busiest airport. He is known to be a generous philanthropist, coming in at the top three most generous corporate donors in India (as reported by China's Hurun Report in 2013).

NIKOLA TESLA: Born in Serbia in 1856, Tesla became one of the most prominent engineers and inventors of his day, although Thomas Edison purported to steal most of Tesla's thunder through the use of better funding and better marketing techniques. It was actually Tesla, not Edison, who sold the patent rights of alternating-current machinery to George Westinghouse.

ECKHART TOLLE: Born Ulrich Leonard Tölle, he is best known for writing *The Power of Now* and *A New Earth*, which sold three million and five million copies, respectively, in North America by 2009. Tolle has said that he was chronically depressed for much of his life but went through a transformation of sorts when he was 29. In 2008, he appeared with Oprah Winfrey in a series of televised workshops in which over 35 million people participated.

NEALE DONALD WALSCH: The first book in Walsch's 10-book series (*Conversations with God*) became a *New York Times* bestseller along with six of his other 28 published books. His work has been translated into 37 languages. Walsch created Humanity's Team, a movement emphasizing that we are all one with God and life.

BIBLIOGRAPHY

Andersen, U.S. *Three Magic Words: The Key to Power, Peace and Plenty.* Chatsworth, CA: Wilshire Book Company, 1977.

Berg, Michael. *Secrets of the Zohar: Stories and Meditations to Awaken the Heart.* Los Angeles: Kabbalah Publishing, 2007.

_____. *Becoming Like God: Our Ultimate Destiny.* Los Angeles: Kabbalah Publishing, 2010.

Berg, Yehuda. *The 72 Names of God Meditation Book: Technology for the Soul.* Los Angeles: Kabbalah Publishing, 2004.

Braden, Gregg. *The Divine Matrix: Bridging Time, Space, Miracles, and Belief.* Carlsbad, CA: Hay House Inc., 2008.

Hamilton, Laird. *Force of Nature: Mind, Body, Soul, And, of Course, Surfing.* Emmaus, PA: Rodale Books, 2010.

Hawkins, David R. *The Discovery: Revealing the Presence of God in Your Life* (audiobook). Wheeling, IL: Nightingale-Conant, 2014.

Millman, Dan. *Way of the Peaceful Warrior: A Book That Changes Lives.* Novato, CA: HJ Kramer, 2006.

Moorjani, Anita. *Dying To Be Me: My Journey from Cancer, to Near Death, to True Healing.* Carlsbad, CA: Hay House Inc., 2014.

Tolle, Eckhart. *The Power of Now: A Guide to Spiritual Enlightenment.* Novato, CA: New World Library, 2004.

_____. *A New Earth: Awakening to Your Life's Purpose.* Westminster, London: Penguin, 2008.

Walsch, Neale Donald. *Conversations with God: An Uncommon Dialogue* (Books 1-4). New York: G. P. Putnam's Sons, 1996.

Made in United States
North Haven, CT
21 February 2022